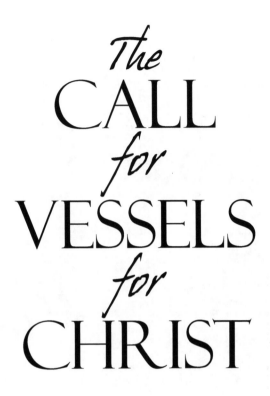

The
CALL
for
VESSELS
for
CHRIST

PAUL PHILLIPS

authorHOUSE

AuthorHouse™
1663 Liberty Drive
Bloomington, IN 47403
www.authorhouse.com
Phone: 833-262-8899

Published by AuthorHouse   03/07/2022

ISBN: 978-1-6655-4978-3 (sc)
ISBN: 978-1-6655-4977-6 (e)

Print information available on the last page.

Any people depicted in stock imagery provided by Getty Images are models, and such images are being used for illustrative purposes only. Certain stock imagery © Getty Images.

Scripture quotations marked KJV are from the Holy Bible, King James Version (Authorized Version). First published in 1611. Quoted from the KJV Classic Reference Bible, Copyright © 1983 by The Zondervan Corporation.

Scripture quotations marked NKJV are taken from the New King James Version. Copyright © 1982 by Thomas Nelson, Inc. Used by permission. All rights reserved.

Scripture quotations marked NIV are taken from the Holy Bible, New International Version®. NIV®. Copyright © 1973, 1978, 1984 by International Bible Society. Used by permission of Zondervan. All rights reserved. [Biblica]

Unless otherwise indicated, all scripture quotations are from The Holy Bible, English Standard Version® (ESV®). Copyright ©2001 by Crossway Bibles, a division of Good News Publishers. Used by permission. All rights reserved.

Scripture quotations marked NLT are taken from the Holy Bible, New Living Translation, copyright © 1996, 2004, 2007. Used by permission of Tyndale House Publishers, Inc. Carol Stream, Illinois 60188. All rights reserved. Website

Scripture taken from the New Century Version®. Copyright © 2005 by Thomas Nelson. Used by permission. All rights reserved.

This book is printed on acid-free paper.

To:

From:

Date:

CONTENTS

ACKNOWLEDGMENTS

I would like to express my sincere appreciation to my excellent team at Authorhouse Publishing, for their vision, inspiration and encouragement in seeing this project come into existence. To those who are dedicated to spreading this message and to the many who are seeking their Calling and fulfilling their purpose in life and desiring to become Vessels for Christ, I am truly grateful.

I dedicate this book to my fifteen Heartbeats

First, giving a very distinct honor to the almighty God who is and will always be the head of my life. Without You Lord in my life, I am nothing more than a sinking Vessel out in an open sea.

To my beautiful and lovely wife of over thirty-five glorious years and my (BFF) Best Friend Forever for over thirty-eight years, Elaina, you are my rock. For over half of my life, through everything, I have ever experienced or been through(The good times and the bad), you have always had my back and have stood by my side. You prayed for me and encouraged me to smile during times when my entire body was in extreme pain. You encouraged me to get up and walk just a little bit further during times when I felt I could barely stand. You encouraged me to stand and speak in front of multitudes of people during times when my body was so weak. You have loved on me and pushed me to do greater things in life and for this, I will forever give you my heart. You are virtuous and the true example of a Proverbs 31 Women! You will always and forever be my darling darling baby and my sweet and tender love. Elaina, I love you and I always will, Paul.

To my three beautiful daughters, Tanisha, Jocelyn, Amber. From the times you gave me butterfly kisses before bedtime prayers until now as mature grown Women of God, you three women have always been ready to give Daddy a hug and a big smile. Daddy is so proud of the anointed women of God you have become. I thank you for always being ready to pray for me and being my inspiration to strive forward. Tanisha, Jocelyn and Amber, I'll always love you till the end, Daddy.

To my three sons(in-laws), Julius, Garland and Michael who are my armor bearers. I thank you three men for being the mighty Vessels God has called you to be. God has a lot instore for you three men. I Thank God for you stepping up to the plate as being the head, the protector and supporter of your household, but most of all loving and protecting my three daughters and seven grandchildren and covering them in prayer. Please continue to keep me covered through prayers as well but most of all keep the family growing closer to Christ. Julius, Garland and Michael, I will always love you, Dad(Pops).

To my seven grandchildren, Julius Jr., Johnathan, Jeremiah, Joshua, Joseph, Amina and Nia who are the loves of my life. The number seven represents perfection in the Bible. I thank you for the love, unlimited hugs and kisses that only a PaPa could truly appreciate. From the times your Moms laid you on my chest as infants until now, you seven have always been the only ones who could truly make PaPa smile and tear up without you even saying a word. There are going to be some rough times throughout life but if you treat people right, pray and stay under God's covering, you can do and make it through anything. Always remember that with God all things are possible.

You Seven are True Vessels of GOD in the Making!!!
Love Always,
Your PaPa

THE CALL
FOR VESSELS

THE POWER WITHIN A VESSEL

love being around the mountains, huge bodies of water, lakes, rivers or ponds, it does not matter to me, I love the great outdoors. Besides being closer to family, these were perhaps the things that most attracted us when my wife and I decided to move from Texas to Tennessee. Tennessee has a lot of those out door features, but what we really enjoy is sitting on the banks of the Cumberland River which runs directly through the heart of the state.

Often times, especially during the mornings, folks would come from near and far to get a great view and watch in amazement these large barges some would seem to stretch over a quarter of a mile long carrying tons of supplies that would arrive and occasionally stop along its journey to pick up a load or to drop one off, and then once again it would disappear around the bends and corners of this mighty Cumberland River heading off to its next destination.

But, what really caught my attention was not so much as the magnitude, size and importance of these huge barges as to the fact that these huge barges could be pushed and manipulated by such a very small vessel, the Tug Boat.

The Tug Boat is a small vessel, dirty and is always behind the barges. It's only job and objective is to push and provide power and guidance to the barges and to make sure they made it safely to their destinations on time. Even though the tug boat is considered small and seemingly unimportant, but without the use of its power and it's force pushing the barges from behind, the barges would drift without direction or purpose.

You may consider yourself to be small and unimportant as the tug boat and even at times finding yourself drifting throughout life without direction or purpose, but the scripture will remind you that you were chosen with a purpose while you were in Him(Ephesians 1:4kjv)and chosen as His own(Ephesians 1:11kjv). He knew us and had us on His mind before we existed in fact He knew us before the world even existed. You are valuable and needed and can be used as a Vessel unto honour for Christ in so many ways. God has a Plan and your life has Purpose!

Ok, you may not have a theological or doctrinal degree, you may not even have total knowledge of the Bible, but you are valuable and essentially needed for the kingdom. Just like the tug boat, small, but it was required. Just like the small tug boat seemingly unimportant, you are important not only here on earth but also important to the kingdom of God!

The huge vessels received power from behind from the tug boat. You will receive power from above from The Holy Spirit! The huge vessels depended upon the tug boat for strength to move forward, The Holy Spirit will give you strength to overcome and push aside any obstacle that comes your way allowing you to move forward.

God's desire is to make us all, a Vessel. One who is sanctified, baptized, and filled with the Holy Spirit, ready and prepared to go out and to perform every good works (2Tim. 2:21-22 kjv) according to His plans. The word "Holy" means "separate, set apart, one of a kind" defining what kind of spirit it is, God is a Holy Spirit!

Wow, to be filled with the Holy Spirit spreading God's Word is so wonderful and awesome that when the spirit hits you and becomes personal in your lifestyle, most times you don't even realize God is using you for His glory and you are fulfilling your purpose in life at the same time!

You may say to yourself, "Yes, I am saved" ok, that's fine, but where is the evidence that you have received the baptism of the Holy

Spirit(Holy Ghost)? Many believers sitting right there in the church today have been a member there their whole lives and were saved many years ago. But, I sincerely ask you the question, and you ask yourself the same question, "Have you received the baptism of the Holy Ghost since you have been saved?" Many people may not even know who the Holy Ghost is and that is probably why Apostle Paul questioned the disciples:

> And he said unto them, Have ye received the Holy Ghost since ye believed? Acts: 19:2 KJV

"Have ye received the Holy Ghost since
ye believed?" (Acts 19:2 kjv)

Every servant in the Bible that came in contact with Jesus had an encounter with the Holy Spirit. Saul had an encounter on his way to Damascus, Moses had an encounter on Mt Horeb in front of a burning bush when he said to the Lord, "Please, show me Your glory" I want more of You, Elisha asked for a double portion of the spirit that was upon Elijah-The Holy Spirit.

Apostle Paul knew that the disciples were saved, but he wanted to know if they had received the Baptism of the Holy Spirit indicating that there are two different things.

He was trying to get them the understand that they needed more than being saved, they needed the power of the Holy Spirit! Being saved requires maturity and growth so that when you receive the Holy Spirit, you will be more able to utilize the God given gifts He has given you. You may say, "Yes, I am saved" ok, but where is the evidence that you have received the baptism of the Holy Spirit?

I was saved many years before showing any evidence of receiving the Holy Ghost but, one day during our weekly prayer meeting the Holy Spirit fell upon me and hit me like a brick wall.

Just like when Apostle Paul laid his hand upon the Disciples head and they were filled with the Holy Ghost:

"And when Paul had laid his hands upon them, the Holy Spirit came on them; and they spake with tongues, and prophesied" (Acts 19:6 KJV).

The Holy Ghost fell upon me in a like manner. Now, I have always loved the Lord but I knew that there was more to it and I wanted it and I wanted it bad. I wanted to be filled with the Holy Spirit with evidence of being filled with it! During the prayer meeting our Minister knew of my hearts desires of wanting the Holy Spirit walked across the prayer room and sat next to me and laid his hand over the top of my head. He began to pray in the Spirit and before I knew it I was out like a lightbulb.

When I woke up, I was speaking in an unknown language which I had no clue as to what I was saying but God knew and that's all that mattered! This had become my personal code or language with the Father that only He understood.

Now, before we reflect on how I received the Holy Spirit with evidence of speaking in tongues or even being used as a Vessel for Christ for that matters, let's take a look at the church itself. Why is it that one church believes that, "We only speak in tongues when an interpreter is available while another church is saying, "We speak in tongues during prophesies and praying" and the church down the street teaches and believes that praying and speaking in tongues is not even allowed during the service times, they prefer that you do that at home?" Why is that? Why are there so many guidelines and so many rules? There is no wonder as to why so many people are confused. Confusion is a dangerous thing especially within the church. With confusion comes doubt. People begin to doubt what they are hearing, they begin to doubt things even written in the Bible, and where did all this doubting begin, right there with the division of the church.

What do you believe or what is your stance on the issues of Intercessory Prayer and speaking in tongues? Well, Let's take a look at what it says in the book of Acts.

"And when the day of Pentecost was fully come, they were all with one accord in one place. And suddenly there came a sound from heaven as of a rushing mighty wind, and it filled all the house where they were sitting. And there appeared unto them cloven tongues like as of fire, and it sat upon each of them. And they were all filled with the Holy Ghost, and began to speak with other tongues, as the Spirit gave them utterance" (Acts 2:1-4 KJV).

The Bible says that speaking in tongues is initial evidence or sign of having the baptism of the Holy Ghost. In regards to intercessory Praying during church or at home, a lot of times when we are praying, we focus on praying for certain things or certain people when we unknowingly should be praying elsewhere. Apostle Paul wrote, "We know not what we should

> We all need to be on the same team because we are all serving the same God!

pray but, the Spirit itself maketh intercession for us with groanings which cannot be uttered"(Romans 8:26). Apostle Paul was not saying that we do not know how to pray but that the Holy Spirit will intercede for us with wordless groanings and guide our prayers in the right direction.

Whatever the case may be, we as the body of Christ need to be on the same team when it comes to communicating with the Father and our prayers being heard because we are all serving the same God. I'm telling you that the same God who protected Daniel in the lion's den, who protected Shadrach, Meshach and Abednego in the fiery furnace is the same God that dwells within you and I. Yes, the same God dealing with you is the same God who is dealing with me and we are all trying to make it into the same Heaven, Amen? Why don't we just work harder on being on the same team?

One thing about a team is that you have to get into formation and stay there. Everyone has a duty and a job to do. Just like the quarterback of a football team's job is to guide the team and deliver the ball, the pastors job is to guide the church, deliver the Word of God and catapult believers into the next level. We as the body of Christ are on the same team pushing each day towards one goal, to make it into heaven.

Now, getting back to our discussion with emphasis on the Holy Spirit(Holy Ghost) and supernatural intercession. Now, before you can have intimacy with the Father, you must first know who the Holy Spirit is. First, the Holy Spirit is a person with feelings. A person who can be sad, happy and so on. The Holy Spirit is the third Person of (God) the Holy Trinity consisting of The Father, Son, and Holy Spirit. The Holy Spirit is simply a powerful part of who God is. We need the Holy Spirit in our life and within us in order for us to become who God created us to be. Without being filled with the Holy Ghost and it dwelling in us, we are powerless to do anything.

Many believers like myself will show evidence of being filled with the Holy Ghost by speaking and praying in the spirit like those as mentioned in the above scripture from the book of Acts. The gift of speaking in tongues is like I said, "a gift" and as a Vessel of Christ you should respect it as a precious endowment.

When you allow yourself to be used as a vessel for Christ, there is a special power that will come upon you unlike anything you have ever experienced in your life. A power that can get you out of sin and keep sin from completely destroying your life. It's a power that can change a person's mind and have them to serve God and it's the Power of the Holy Ghost!

The Power of the Holy Ghost is a power from God that is more valuable than money, riches or gold, it's always on time and helps you fulfill all desires and purposes God has for you and more!

Even if your desires in life does not line up with God's plan, He will still use every one of us, every aspect in us in some capacity or another for His glory. Questions are, "Are you ready" and "which way do you want to be used" by Him?" It does not matter if you are a Doctor, a Lawyer, unemployed or even homeless, the Bible says that at the name of Jesus every knee shall bow and every tongue shall confess that Jesus Christ is Lord and His desire for you and I is to become a Vessel, one who is baptized and filled with the Holy Spirit! The Holy Spirit is an absolute necessity in our lives today especially as followers of Christ, no doubt.

We all together are part of Christ body and you are part of this body. The body of Christ need vessels and is calling for believers to stand up and speak out to the world that CHRIST IS LORD and that they will walk according to their SPIRITUAL CALLING! The Power within a Spiritual Vessel is the Holy Spirit! Who is this vessel I am talking about and who I am referring to? WELL, THIS VESSEL I AM REFERRING TO IS, YOU, YES YOU!

Are you ready to become that Vessel for Christ, then get ready, put your boots on and let's go!

PART I

THE FUNDAMENTAL OF VESSELS

A Vessel of Honor is one who openly exemplifies
and carries out the purposeful will of God
under the leadership of His son Jesus Christ.

1

>> >> >> >> >> >> << << << << << << <<

THE CALL FOR VESSELS

"I am the LORD; I have called you in righteousness;
I will take you by the hand and keep you; I
will give you as a covenant for the people, a
light for the nations" (Isaiah 42:6 ESV).

et me start by asking you a question, do you believe that you have a Spiritual calling on your life, by God? More than likely the answer is a definite, YES! But, at times you may feel that you have either not quite fully stepped into your calling or even worse, you have missed your calling completely.

First off, what is your Spiritual Calling? Think about it like this. When you receive your driver's license you will see that it identifies who you are: it shows your picture, name, address and what class of driving you are qualified to drive.

Your Spiritual Calling is your personal calling card. It identifies who you are as a person and the purposeful plan God has for you, nothing else. God is the only one who can match the calling in your life with your purpose. God has given each of us a Spiritual calling but the terrible thing about it is that for many of us we have either failed to utilize our calling to its fullest potential or worse we have completely forgotten the benefits and availability of what God has given to us. This simply reveals that there is a lack of knowledge of who you are called to be, that's not good.

No matter what the reason is, God still loves you dearly and you were called by Him to do good works! It may take someone reminding you of your Spiritual Calling or in an extreme case it may take someone searching you out through a crowd grabbing on you saying, "Come on, you are the one I am looking for" letting you know that there is a special calling upon your life.

That is an extreme case but it was the case for a young boy by the name of David. Let's take a look as to how David was searched out from others to serve in the capacity of what God called for him.

We find that after Saul was rejected to be king (1 Sam. 15:9) because of his disobedience, The Lord appointed Samuel to search out and find a future King of Israel among Jesse's eight sons (1 Samuel 16:1kjv). Samuel interviewed each of Jesse's sons one by one and could not find a single person who was fit to be a future King.

CHOSEN AMONG MANY

"Again, Jesse made seven of his sons to pass
before Samuel. And Samuel said unto Jesse, The
Lord hath not chosen these"(1 Samuel 16:10 kjv)

Samuel was crushed over the fact that God had rejected Saul to be King but being assured of his assignment to find a future king among Jesse's eight sons he asked if all his sons had been seen and interviewed?

Jesse said, "There remained the youngest who keeps the sheep" (1 Samuel 16:11 kjv). Now, here comes the introduction of a future king, a mighty warrior, a writer of many psalms, a boy by the name of David.

David, being a young shepherd boy looked rough, without a beautiful countenance and the least likely to be chosen by Samuel to be a future king, but when Samuel saw little David he did not have to look any further, the Lord said, "Arise, anoint him: for this is he"(1

Samuel 16:12 ASV). The Bible says, "Feed my sheep" as you can see here, God was preparing David to feed His people as a youthful shepherd.

Samuel anointed David and the Spirit of the Lord came upon him to be a future king of Israel on the spot, a high school boy.

Now, I am sure that David's older brothers even Jesse his father were standing around wondering to themselves, "You have got to be kidding, the shepherd boy?" David's brothers saw a shepherd boy, but God saw a future King of Israel.

This shows that even being considered the least among many, God will always see the best in you. When God calls you, you may not always know what's coming next in your life. Other folks may have given up on you and at times there seems to be no hope for you and you are three seconds from throwing in the towel but, great news, when everyone around you only sees the worst in you, the good Lord will stand before you and will always see the best in you. He knows your yesterday, today, tomorrow, He knows your year from now, He knows your entire life, you are in God's hand!

> "For the Lord seeth not as man seeth; for man looketh on the outward appearance, but the Lord looketh on the heart."
> (1Samuel 16:7 KJV)

Listen here my dear reader, He did not bring you this far to leave you. God knew that David was anointed and that he had a calling on his life even at the time being a young rough looking shepherd boy. David was called to be a future King and a Vessel of God when he was only but a youth but, he would not serve as king until the age of thirty.

One of the worse things in life is to wake up each day without a purpose. To go throughout life with no expectations or goals and to live each day with nothing to do. Knowing God's calling upon your life provides you with stability and gives you clear direction in life. You might say, "OK, I know and understand that but, how do I discover God's calling on my life?" Well, I can offer only a few suggestions:

3

1. Think about *what* are you really passionate about and how it can please God? What are the things that give you energy and pleasure in doing? Maybe you enjoy *helping people* or you enjoy *volunteering* for example.
2. Think about *ways* in which you can utilize helping people to its fullest extent. First, pay attention to the people around you. You may see a neighbor struggling carrying something heavy or perhaps checking on the elderly and making short visits. Believe me, any act of kindness and helping will be appreciated. In what ways can you best utilize the things you are called to do in life?
3. Think about *where* would you have the greatest chance to share your gifts which would give you the best opportunity to show love and compassion toward others. Churches are a great place to volunteer and hospitals are always in need of additional help. Do you know how much of an impact you can make on someone's life by simply showing a smile? Your smile can brighten a sadden heart, believe me.

Now, let me explain something to you. Anybody can have a calling on their life but there is a difference between having a calling on your life and that of having a Spiritual calling on your life. You can have a calling on your life for example by being a great cook or a talented dancer but the difference is that when you have a spiritual calling upon your life, God's anointing is involved and in the midst of it.

Now, regarding a Vessel. The definition of a vessel is "any type of watercraft, including non-displacement craft and seaplane used or capable of being used as a means of carrying or transportation."

We are God's chosen vessels and He has chosen us to carry out His Will and that purposeful plan He has designed for our lives. When a true Vessel of Christ wakes in the morning and places his feet on the floor, the enemy cries and yells out of fear, "OH NO, HE'S UP AGAIN!" The enemy knows that something is about to take place, something super natural is about to happen and that we are ready to step out and minister a Word, ready to make a difference in someone's life and are ready and prepared to be used by God in any capacity He chooses.

The Good Lord wants and desires for you and I to be that Vessel! The question again is, "Are you willing and ready?"

You may feel that you are not qualified or that you are unworthy to be used by God or that you will do those things a little bit later in life.

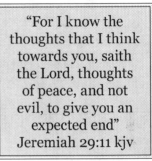

"For I know the thoughts that I think towards you, saith the Lord, thoughts of peace, and not evil, to give you an expected end"
Jeremiah 29:11 kjv

First of all, who promised you tomorrow? That is exactly what Satan wants you to believe (*I can put things off until tomorrow*). Believe me when I say to you that God can use anybody, anytime, anywhere, or anything for His glory including a donkey or a rock!

God does not need anything from us but, we need everything from Him! The point I am trying to make here is that no matter what circumstances you may be going through in life, no matter what people may think of you, God can use you for His glory no matter who you are or what you may have done. Take for example:

<u>King David</u>, who was the great grandson of Ruth and Boaz was a man after God's own heart. But even then he had his own issues. David caused many wars and had multiple affairs, but God still used him in a mighty way.

This was a man who had killed over 10,000 men winning many battles but David helped Israel to become a formidable nation. This reminds us to not let our past dictate our future. As a youth David was used to kill Goliath, he had an affair with Bathsheba but God used David to write many Psalms and eventually becoming King of Israel, such a talented poet he was.

Take for example Moses, who was the son of Amram and Jochebed. He was a murderer and a stutterer but, God used Moses's mouth (*his least likely quality*) to speak to Pharoah and to His people. God used Moses and his staff to part the Red Sea and to deliver and lead His people out of captivity and bondage in Egypt to the Promise Land, what a guy.

Consider Rahab, she was a prostitute but was only one of the five women who were actually mentioned in Matthew's genealogy of Jesus Christ. God used her to hide two spies from death as she hid them in the safety of her rooftop while they searched out the land of Jericho in order for Israel to take control of Canaan (Joshua 2:1-24 kjv). Quick thinking Rahab.

Your past(*which you can't do anything about*) does not matter to God as much as your future. If you are reading this, that means that you have time to make a difference in your life and in someone else's life as well. At this present moment you are in the perfect position to be used as a Vessel for Christ which for many of us will require a lot of God's grace and mercy, starting with me. Grace is the unmerited favour of God and Mercy is the compassion or forgiveness shown toward others whom it is within one's power to punish or harm them.

> We are all in need of God's grace and mercy in our lives today

To be truthful about it my dear reader, we are all in need of God's grace and mercy in our lives today! God's grace will give us the confidence we need in knowing that we have a purpose in fulfilling our calling and His mercies is the loving kindness we need when applying our calling in life towards others, right?

God is the provider of both grace and mercy. This will show that you are an open book allowing God to work through you and that you are ready to be a Vessel! The question is, and I will go back to the beginning of our conversation and ask again "Are you ready to accept the challenge and in agreement with Him?"

LEAST LIKELY TO MOST VALUABLE

I think that the greatest example of being a father was shown to me through my own father. Before retiring, my father worked as a machine operator for over forty years at The Cincinnati Milacron where he never missed a day when there was work available.

During the times when the company had its yearly shutdown we as a family would travel to Fremont Ohio to fish for the White Bass that made a yearly run through the Sandusky River to spawn. There would be times when my father, my mother, my little brother and myself would catch so many fish that we ended up giving coolers full of them away.

I'm talking about bringing home two to three hundred fish. We ate White Bass with grits for breakfast, we ate White Bass with fries for lunch and we ate White Bass, cornbread and a salad for dinner. Believe me, I have had my fill of fish and even today I cringe when I see a White Bass in the stores grocery freezer case.

Despite how I feel about White Bass, I will never forget my father's consistency in providing for our family. Every day he would come home from work wearing dirty clothes full of machine oil from head to toe. After work he and his other oil covered coworkers would gather in the companies parking lot and talk about the day's activities.

> Who hath saved us, and called us with an holy calling, not according to our works, but according to His own purpose and grace, which was given us in Christ Jesus before the world began.
> (2 Timothy 1:9 KJV)

But, there was this one guy who stood out from all the other coworkers. He had on the same uniform as the others, same educational level as the rest, he even lived in the same neighborhood as all the rest but he stood out like a sore thumb. His clothes and shoes were clean, nice haircut and all.

I asked my Dad who he was and he said that we would talk about it a little later. Later on that night, my Dad actually approached me and said that he wanted to talk to me about this guy who stood out from the crowd whose name was Thomas.

My Dad said: "Thomas is different. Even though he is considered a bit lazy, well very lazy, always hiding in the bathroom stalls, behind the buildings doing God knows what, but he is still able to keep a job for over thirty-two years and is probably considered very valuable to the company."

I said "Wow, how could this possibly be, especially being lazy like that?"

"Well" my Dad explained, "Junior, you know that we work at a multi-billion dollar a year company, right?"

I said, "Yes."

"Anyway we get major projects every three weeks or so. Each time a new project comes in, the company will have Thomas to work on that project for at least one week before the initial work would start.

The reason being is that the supervisors know that even though Thomas is considered by many as being the laziest person in the entire company, that lazy spirit of his could be used in a positive way.

By being lazy, Thomas could find the easiest, quickest, and most efficient way to perform a project, overall saving the company time and money. He was allowed to work on every new project before anyone else did. Thomas had gained respect and had become a valuable asset to the company." I looked at my Dad wondering how could a spirit of laziness become so valuable and such a talent but it did.

Thomas had a calling on his life, not to be lazy of course, but he unlike anyone else could find unique and distinct ways to save valuable money and time not only at home but also at work! Also, unknown to everybody else, Thomas enjoyed doing what he was doing and was probably the only employee smiling while working.

Remember my dear reader that Satan has an assignment as well and that is to try to interfere what God has for you but also remember that God can use even a negative talent of yours to be used in a positive manner.

God has chosen you and I for a specific assignment: to serve him, to be used by Him and to fulfill His purpose and promises but most of all, to bomb bard the heavens with Saints that He may be Glorified!

GRACE

Now, I truly believe that God created man and woman with natural talents. These are features of God's grace He has invested in us. Before moving to Tennessee my wife and I belonged to a church that held yearly conferences where it was not uncommon to have two to three thousand believers in attendance.

During the days there would be small meetings or small conferences touching on such topics as "The Family," "The coming of Christ," "Baptism" etc., whereby individuals could attend before the main meeting to be held later that evening.

After the evening meeting we would all have a late-night snack and believe me the lines were long. But everything was organized and the lines went rather fast. There was one lady who was in charge of this hospitality, her name was Giselle.

You would not have known it but providing hospitality to over three thousand people took a lot of preparation, talent and the grace of God. Nobody knew it but, Giselle had prepared for this event months and months in advance, she appointed people to serve, appointed people to constantly keep food available and had appointed a clean-up crew so that things would run smoothly.

While the workers she had appointed were tired and wore out, Giselle continued working wherever she was needed with a smile and after it was over and people were fed, place was clean and time for sleep, she would stay and read her Bible for a while.

If you want a double portion of what God is offering to you my dear reader, it is going to require sacrifice, commitment and dedication. You must be willing to stay up when everyone else has gone to sleep. You must be able to press forward and continue fighting, when everyone else has given up. You have to remind yourself to GET UP, THE FIGHT IS NOT OVER YET!

Generosity was Giselle's natural talent and serving others was her Spiritual Calling as she would often say with a smile, "This could not have done this without the grace of God."

Now as you can see, the overall definition of a Spiritual Calling is when you can actually step into your destiny God has designed and intended

> Remember, what God has for you, it is for you!

specifically just for you and God is in the midst of it. You enjoy and are excited about what you are doing and you still have compassion towards others while doing it! Remember, what God has for you, it is for you!

A lot of times we find ourselves doing things we enjoy doing but after a year or so the thrill of it is gone. That was never your Spiritual calling from the beginning. When God places you into what He designed for you to do, you will do it with pleasure and money will be an afterthought.

STEP INTO IT

When I was about fourteen years of age, my Uncle Clarence came to Ohio for a visit. He was an architect by profession but his true passion was photography. I admired him during the times when he would carefully focus his camera lens to the precise settings and held his head a certain way to get that one perfect shot. I even heard him once say to himself, "Oh, I missed it." Yeah, I admired him but, one year he got on me for something I did or did not do.

It was a year when we were attending a family funeral, and as usual my Uncle Clarence was taking pictures and I asked if I could work along beside him in taking pictures. He looked at me and asked, "Are you serious about taking pictures?" I said with enthusiasm, "yes!"

As the funeral service was going about I felt important as we both walked around the entire funeral home taking hundreds of pictures. After a while, I decided to take a personal break and I just stop taking pictures.

My Uncle came to me and asked "If there was a problem as to why I stopped photographing and taking pictures?" I'm getting ready to be taught a valuable lesson. Me being only fifteen or so replied, "Uncle Clarence, I just wanted to take a break." He looked at me with that half-smile and half-grin of his and said, "Look here doc, if you are going to be a photographer taking pictures, then take the pictures, because if you miss that one shot, that money shot, that once in a lifetime moment in time is gone, brother it is gone forever." Just those few words put such conviction in my heart and for one of the first times in my life, I took something serious.

I think that my feelings were hurt more from disappointing my uncle than actually missing a once in a lifetime picture. Many years after that incident, I can still hear his voice as I am often called upon to take professional photographs and yes often times people will ask if it's ok for them to assist me. I realized that photography was one of my callings in life that I still enjoy doing to this day.

It shows that sometimes we may have a calling on our life but have missed the shot. That once in a lifetime opportunity of fulfilling what God called you to do, you missed the money shot. Believe me, it's not too late, there are a few seconds left on the clock or we will just have to go into overtime. You still have time to step into you calling even if you have to stop doing what you are doing at the present moment to seek the Lord in prayer for guidance.

He says:

> "Call unto Me, and I will answer thee, and shew thee
> great and mighty things, which thou knowest not"
> (Jeremiah 33:3 KJV).

Whatever your calling in life may be, the sooner you realize it and step into it, the better off you will be. When you fail to recognize your calling in life you will fall to the call of man rather than that of God, now that's not good at all, is it?

Reflection and Relevant Questions

1. In this chapter, we talked about being a chosen Vessel for Christ and your Spiritual Calling. In what capacities do you feel that you are Called and what areas are you being used as a Vessel for Christ?

2. David was considered the least among his many brothers chosen to be King (Read Luke 9:48 KJV) "For he that is least among you all, the same shall be great." What does this verse mean to you? Give an example of how you were chosen among many others (maybe it was for a job promotion, a school event, etc.) as it applies to your own life.

3. How important is it to you that you are in alignment with God's purpose for your life?

   a. Do you at times find it hard to stay in Gods Will or do you find certain people becoming a hindrance to you? Spend a moment seeking God in prayer to give you the courage to overcome these hindrances.

   b. Think about something. You were given a firm foundation in Christianity, you have a personal relationship with God, describe what is keeping you grounded.

2

»»»»»»» «««««««

YOU ARE CHOSEN

But ye are a chosen generation, a royal priesthood,
a holy nation, a peculiar people; that ye should
shew forth the praises of him who hath called
you out of darkness into his marvelous light;
(1 Peter 2:9 KJV).

have been a Chaplain for many years working at various hospitals, first at The Bethesda Hospital located in Cincinnati Ohio, then at the UT Tyler Hospital located in Tyler Texas. If you have ever worked in any capacity within the health care profession, you already know a head of time that the job does not come easy.

My only job as an entry level chaplain at that time was to deliver hospital information to the patient mailboxes. Many times I would place a personal prayer track from our local church in their mailboxes for them to read as well.

After about three months or so I was allowed to make short patient visits where I was allowed to sit and talk with them which I found to be very rewarding. This gave me the opportunity to pray with patients, to share my own personal testimony, to provide encouragement and to read the Word of God to them.

As I had gotten more proficient in my duties, I was eventually placed on a specific floor and wouldn't you know it, (The Kidney Transplant floor). Have you ever wondered how God will send you back to minister at the same place where you had a personal health issue or battled a trial in your own life?

In addition to that, I was on call for patients and family members who were in need of immediate counseling or prayer especially in regards to dialysis, transplant procedures things which I was already familiar with and I could speak from a patients point of view. There were many times when I would be called in, it could have been midnight or during our dinner time but whatever the case was, I had to go.

> "For the Holy Ghost shall teach you in the same hour what ye ought to say" Luke 12:12 kjv

But, I have to admit that there were many times when a patient's family member would ask me for my opinion and even from a patients point of view, I had no answer. I would simply respond by saying, "I'm not sure but, let me check with another chaplain, pray on it and I will have a response for you within an hour."

> "For the Holy Ghost shall teach you in the
> same hour what ye ought to say"
> (Luke 12:12 KJV).

I have found that calling upon the Lord for wisdom as opposed to depending on my own experience and opinions to be the best and honest way of dealing with difficult situations. Many of those same family members responded with a smile by saying, "Thank you for being honest with us."

MY FIRST LOVE

Being a Vessel for Christ, you must first love Christ with all your heart and you must be born again! Meaning that Christ must live in you and you must be water baptized making sure of your salvation.

Besides that, how can you be a Vessel for Christ if you are not born again?

You may not even know Christ, and you may not be able to recognize his voice but God knows His sheep. You may have done what you consider as some of the most terrible things in your past and you feel that God has forgotten all about you, such is not the case. God loves you and He knows His sheep and will stop you right in your tracks and give your life a complete

> Jesus said unto him, Thou shalt love the Lord thy God with all thy heart, and with all thy soul, and with all thy mind.
> Matthew 22:37 KJV

turnaround. OK you ask, "What is a turnaround?" Well, let's look at one of God's servants who at first was the complete opposite person of who God planned for him to be and like I said, "God knows His sheep" but he still needed a turnaround.

SAUL'S CONVERSION

It is of upmost importance to know Saul of Tarsus(Paul), a man who was out to persecute of all people, the Christians and Jews, a guy simply wanting to kill them all(Acts 9:1). Because, if you don't know Saul as the religious terrorist and persecutor of Christians, then it will be hard for you to truly appreciate and understand him as Paul one of the Apostles of Jesus Christ.

Now, Saul was simply a terrible person and he needed a total over haul of his heart and a spiritual turn around in order for God to use him. On his way to Damascus with the cruel intent of destruction and killing Christians, Saul became blind and helpless and it was only then that God was able to speak to him:

"Saul, Saul(Paul) why persecutest thou me?"

Saul needed a total overhaul.

Later on in the same chapter we find Ananias who himself was another disciple of Jesus. The Lord spoke to Ananias regarding Saul saying, "He is a chosen vessel unto me (Acts 9:15 KJV)." Ananias healed Saul of his blindness and Saul began preaching about Christ as his new intent was now to lead Christians and Jews to Christ. In order for God to make all things new in your life, He has to do away with the old things. You may be carrying a heavy load in your life right now, but God is going to turn it around in your favor. Actually, Saul was a chosen vessel even before he knew or realized it himself.

> "But ye shall receive power, after that the Holy Ghost is come upon you: and ye shall be witnesses unto me both in Jerusalem, and in all Judea in Samaria, and unto the uttermost part of the earth" (Acts 1:8 KJV).

During Saul's conversion from being a Christian terrorist to becoming a devout follower of Christ, God changed his name from Saul to Paul. When God changes your name, He may change where you are going and your destination.

All Paul needed was one touch from God and he became a new person and God used his newly ability.

Think about it: Paul was knocked down off his horse and blind for three days deprived of all physical ability but God gave him spiritual ability to transform people, He gave Paul ability to heal and to build people up and was used in a mighty way in the conversion of the Jews to Christianity

So while you are down and off your horse, use the spiritual ability God has given you. Just like Apostle Paul (*who would bring hope to the world*) you also can bring hope to those around you.

To be truthful about it, we all are sinners, and we are in need of a conversion and in need of God's grace and mercies. Question is, "Do you personally have to have a name change or in need of a complete turnaround in your life to follow Christ?" There is something that separates us from the presence of the Lord and there is something that separates us from the Holy Spirit and that one thing is-sin.

I will mention this again, First, you must love Christ with all of your whole heart, then you must have a desire to serve and to be used by him not only here as an earthly vessel but also to the kingdom and lastly, you must love yourself. Believe me, God has given you the spiritual ability to transform people, to heal and to lift people up. You are indeed needed right here right now to bring hope to a dying world!

The Anointing of the Holy Spirit will give you power to overcome the things that are trying to overcome you and supply the grace to carry you through. The Anointing of the Holy Spirit will cause you to love your enemies in a way that while they are cursing you out spreading rumors about you throughout the town, you are in the kitchen cooking them dinner. The Holy Spirit is powerful! One touch from God, the things you used to do, you will never do again.

GOD IS CALLING YOU!

If you don't know it, you know it now that there are people in the world crying out! Crying out for the Word of God, but have no one to share it with them! Crying out desperately wanting to be saved and to be filled with the Holy Ghost but, don't have anyone to lead them in a way in which they can receive it!

God is calling you to be that vessel to go out and share His Word and to lead those desperate souls to Him! Yes, you are that vessel, you are prepared and Yes, you are ready right now! Let me ask you a question or two, "If you saw someone who was hungry would you feed them?" "If you saw someone crying, would you be concerned and stop to help them?" Of course you would.

Don't hesitate in helping God's people where help is needed, that is your Calling! Feed them, Pray for them, lay hands on them and lead them to Christ!

DESTINY

My wife Elaina, once worked as an Activities Director for a local Nursing Home. At that time, I would occasionally make friendly visits to her job where I was permitted to minister, pray, and sit and talk with the many residents who had come from all around the state and from all different walks of life. One particular conversation I remember was with a lady who I believe her to be in her late eighties.

She had been a high school teacher in her younger years but had retired many years ago and was now confined to a wheelchair.

As we began talking, she would on occasion point to various residents giving a brief background of each. One patient she pointed to had retired as a doctor, one who had been the head of the cardiovascular dept, and another she pointed to use to be a janitor.

She eventually turned and looked me straight in the eye and said with a gentle smile, "No matter what we did in life or what path we chose to live, no matter how much education was achieved, there is one destiny we all here have in common and that is when it is all over said and done, we all end up in the same place, a nursing home."

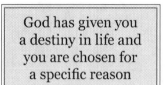

God has given you a destiny in life and you are chosen for a specific reason

My dear reader, God has given you a destiny in life and you are chosen for a specific reason. You are not here just to be here or to take up space. Maybe you have not come to realize or have a complete understanding of your destiny in life and it has become a struggle.

Or perhaps on the other hand, you do have an understanding of your destiny and a specific reason for living but have not quite completely tapped into it just yet. Whatever the case is, God is calling and patiently waiting for you to step into it. No matter what you are going through in your life right now, there is still hope in fulfilling your destiny, it's not too late.

But, before you do anything, first and foremost, seek God and pray for spiritual wisdom! He will guide you in the right direction. Secondly, who knows you best: a parent, a friend, or even a coworker? They just might help you to realize and understand who you are deep inside and that perhaps, you are actually living out your destiny at the present moment.

Knowing who you are changes things. You act differently, think, walk and talk differently. You are rare and you are a special person. In fact, you are so special that there will only be one of you to ever exist.

But, at the same time, always remember, we are a team. Each of us have a specific part to play. The coach will not have the best player on the team running out for coffee during the last moments of the game or the water boy shooting the last shot. The best player is needed throughout the game for a specific purpose and so is the water boy! Each one has their own job to do. We are a team and we have to work and live together!

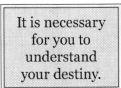

It is necessary for you to understand your destiny.

No matter what part you may play in life, you are important to the team! In the same way, we are all part of God's team, the body of Christ! That is why it is necessary for you to understand the part you play in it, your destiny.

We walk through life experiencing different aspects of it. We have different aspects when it comes to politics, we have different aspects regarding education, we even have different aspects when it comes to religious beliefs.

One thing we all have in common is that we serve a God, but if you are not serving the True and living God, the God of the Heavens and the earth, unlike all ending up in the same place as a nursing home, I'm sorry to say that not all of us will end up in the same place. But as for me and for my house, Yes, we will serve the Lord. The only true and living God, the God who is our Savior and Redeemer and the one who rules the heavens and earth!

A TRUE VESSEL FOR CHRIST

A true Vessel for Christ is one who is prepared under any situation or circumstance and is ready to do the will of God. You may be standing in a grocery line talking with a total stranger, or listening to someone venting out todays frustrations or even meeting and talking with new neighbors, point is, we should never miss an opportunity to minister to someone the

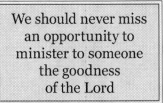

We should never miss an opportunity to minister to someone the goodness of the Lord

goodness of the Lord, take advantage of every opportunity possible!

You never know the impact you play in a person's life until you do what you do for Christ. You don't have to stand behind a podium, you don't have to ride down the street in your car yelling through a loud speaker to make an impact, just be open and be yourself. It's the small things that make the biggest impact.

MAKING AN IMPACT

Let me tell you about a believer I once knew who is now long gone. We called her Elizabeth. She was up in age, quiet but always attended church. She was known for simply passing out church tracks throughout the neighborhood. These tracks were simply a piece of paper maybe two inches by four inches with scriptures and words of encouragement written on them.

One day you might find Elizabeth passing out tracks on one side of town and the next day she would be on the other side of town. On every track she would personally write her name, the churches name and address on them.

She once gave a testimony about the time when she needed to drive forty miles into the next county for an appointment. As she sat in the waiting room she looked over a few chairs and noticed a lady reading what looked like one of the church tracks. She looked closer and realized it was and her name was written on it indicating that she at one time or another personally had passed it out.

She asked the lady where she had gotten the track from and the lady replied, "I got this from a friend who lives fifteen miles in the opposite direction and they both have made plans to attend the church listed on the bottom of it." Elizabeth never identifying herself just smiled wondering how one of her tracks could end up over fifty miles from where she passes them out? You never know the impact you can play on a person's life. It's the little things that make the biggest impacts. God used Elizabeth to be a vessel and that one track could possibly bring hundreds to Christ.

The greatest impacts you may have may not be something you do but rather the investment you put into someone's life especially when it comes to a child's life. The investment in a child may come in the form of offering time, education, encouragement, leadership or simply being there for support.

The early years of our younger generation are the most crucial. It is a time when they comprehend the most and learn basic foundations that will carry them through a lifetime. You can have the biggest influence and make the greatest impact on their life starting right now.

As I mentioned earlier, a true vessel for Christ is one who is always prepared and not afraid to go out into the mission field. They are completely open to do God's Will no matter the cost involved they are ready to make an impact.

Romans 9:21-23 tells us clearly that man was created and formed as a vessel. We are containers of the very presence of God. God does not need anything from us, He calls us to be vessels unto glory, vessels unto honor and vessels unto mercy to contain HIM, that's all. God destined you and I to be containers full of Him and full of the Holy Ghost!

> The Baptism Holy Ghost fire was to come from Jesus Christ Himself

"What? Know ye not that your body is the temple of the Holy Ghost which is in you, which ye have of God, and ye are not your own? For ye are brought with a price: therefore glorify God in your body, and in your spirit, which are God's." 1 Corinthians 6:19-20 KJV

Think about John the Baptist. He was a vessel for Christ speaking about Jesus even before Jesus appeared on the scene or while Jesus was still a child. His message was, "Yes, I baptize you with water, but there is one coming who will baptize you with fire!" As mentioned in the book of Matthews, John the Baptist, baptized people in the waters of the River Jordon, but at the same time he advised them that water was not going to save them that they needed to be saved and baptized with fire. The baptism Holy Ghost fire was to come from Jesus Christ Himself.

Yes my dear reader, I truly believe that the fire of the Holy Ghost is needed in our lives today as followers of Christ. Never forget that you were brought with a price. The price that was paid was to redeem us, to set us free from wrath and the penalties of sin. That shedding of blood by Jesus Christ at Calvary was the cost that was paid to reconcile us back to God.

Reflection and Relevant Questions

1. Read 2nd Chronicles 2:18. Besides Micaiah always giving Ahab bad prophesies, what else could possibly be a reason for Ahab's hatred towards Micaiah?
    a. Why was it so hard for Ahab to listen to Micaiah? Let me ask you a question, "Do you sometimes find it hard to receive bad but honest news (especially regarding your life)from others?
    b. Would you prefer not to hear bad news even if it could save your life, why? Explain.

2. Apostle Paul needed a complete revision and change in his life during his conversion. Name a time during your life when God changed or revised your heart towards Him or towards someone else. How did it affect you and others and were they led to Christ from your turn around? Did it draw you or them closer to Christ? Explain
    a. Saul (before being converted to Paul)was one of the ones who was not only against the Christian church but also had extreme hatred toward the Jews, why is this so, considering the fact that he himself was a Jew? Was he simply following the traditions of his fathers or was there something else involved here? Explain. (read Acts 8:1)
    b. Where was Saul first called Paul and what was his mission for being there? (read Acts 13:1-16)
    c. Even after being converted from Saul to Paul, why did Paul still choose to use his Roman name Saul? (read Romans 11:13)

3. In just a few words, what is your personal definition of a true Vessel of Christ? Do you feel that you are fulfilling the role of being one? Explain.
    a. We understand the purpose of being baptized. Explain the difference of being baptized with water and that of being baptized with fire.

3

>>>>>>>><<<<<<<<<<

GET UNDERSTANDING

Wisdom is the principal thing; therefore get
wisdom: and with all thy getting get understanding.

postle Paul was not only a devout follower of Jesus but,
he was also a teacher. Not just any kind of a teacher
but, he was a teacher who served in the capacity as an
authorized messenger 0f our Lord Jesus Christ. One
of the main points Apostle Paul taught was that we should take a firm
hold on sound teachings of the Word of God and to avoid unbiblical
teachings(2 Timothy 2:16-19kjv).

But, let me ask you something, "How can you really recognize
the true gospel from unbiblical teachings if you have been taught
unbiblical teachings or living a certain way your entire life?" Are you
even capable of recognizing a false teacher? Where do you draw the
line when someone is speaking and they start to waver between what
is of God and what is not, what is right and what is wrong? There has
to be a clear distinction.

I have a cousin who had spent years in college studying electronics
and computer operations. During a particular company meeting a
visiting salesman came and was speaking on this very subject. This
gentleman placed two of their computer parts together stating that

this would solve a major computer issue the entire company was dealing with.

Immediately a red flag arouse in my cousins head and he spoke up explaining that the gentleman had a great idea but within a few months or so it would totally crash the computer system of the entire company. After further testing and getting a full understanding of what the salesman was saying, it was found that my cousin was actually right and the idea was thrown out.

These are times when you need to know for yourself what is right and what is wrong and say, "Wait a minute, that's not what I read or something just don't sound right."

> When you know that you know, and you know you are right, speak up, especially when it comes to defending the Word of God!

The same way it is with the Word of God. When you know that you know, and you know you are right, speak up, especially when it comes to defending the Word of God!

That was the main reason why Apostle Paul was so adamant when it came to sound teachings of the gospel. The importance of reading and studying the word of God for yourself. To have a full comprehension of the Bible so that when you hear the word or speaking the word you can do so with discernment, knowledge and confidence.

UNDERSTANDING THE WORD OF GOD

It was July 1799, when a French soldier happen to be digging a post for their tent in the desert sand, discovered a black slab inscribed with ancient writings near the town of Rosetta which is located about 35 miles east of Alexandria.

The irregularly shaped stone turning out to be the Rosetta Stone (now housed in the British Museum) contained fragments of passages written in three different writings: Greek, Egyptian hieroglyphics and Egyptian.

Through deciphering and having the ability to read the Greek writings it was found that all three writings had the same identical meaning. This would be one of the most important archaeological finds of the nineteenth century because it helped in unlocking the mysteries of the ancient Egyptian writings known as hieroglyphics a written language that had been "dead" for nearly 2000 years. It required putting the three fragments together to unravel the mystery of the Ancient Egyptian hieroglyphic writings.

When I was younger grasping for knowledge, I would find it difficult at times reading and understanding the Bible. Either I would lose interest in the middle of reading or have no clue as to what I had just read. Believe me, it took time, patience, and a lot of prayers to begin understanding and putting the Bible together and really grasping it. For me though, I found that getting a full understanding of the Bible was simply reading it line by line.

In our home, my mother who was and is still to this day a devout Bible scholar who has several translations of the Bible (KJV, NKJV, NIV) lying on the living room table. This made it more confusing to me when reading the different versions of the Bible, but, one thing I came to realize was that even though they were in different translations and versions, the one thing that they all had in common was that they all led to the redemptive story of Jesus Christ.

The Bible tells us to "Trust in the Lord with all thine heart; and lean not unto thine own understanding"(Proverbs 3:5 KJV) because on the night before the cross, He promised to His followers that He would send the Holy Spirit.

> He told them, *"Howbeit when he, the Spirit of truth, is come, he will guide you into all truth: for he shall not speak of himself; but whatsoever he shall hear, that shall he speak: and he will shew you things to come (John 16:13 KJV).*

Yes, The Holy Spirit will give you the understanding you need but, it still amazes me how several people can read the exact same verse and each one can come up with a different perception of what it meant. No, I do not believe that we were meant to understand everything written in the Holy Bible because it was written by men but, it was inspired by the infinite wisdom of God, who can compare to that? But, while we are not promised a complete understanding of everything given to us in scripture, we can have assurance that through the scriptures, we can all understand the things that we need in order for us to follow and be a dedicated vessel for Christ.

> Wherefore I also, after I heard of your faith in the Lord Jesus, and love unto all the saints, cease not to give thanks for you, making mention of you in my prayers; That the God of our Lord Jesus Christ, the Father of glory, may give unto you the spirit of wisdom and revelation in the knowledge of him. The eyes of your understanding being enlightened; that ye may know what is the hope of his calling, and what the riches of the glory of his inheritance in the saints.
> Ephesians 1:15-18 KJV

To tell you the truth, it helps me out a lot when I pray beforehand especially when reading the Bible. *"that the eyes of your understanding be enlightened" (Ephesians 1:18 KJV)*

God will not only give me a better understanding but also clearer thoughts allowing me to totally focus on the Word and my mind won't start drifting off thinking about other things.

Have you ever started reading the Bible and a song would come on or the thought of food would come to mind and all of a sudden you find yourself singing that song or you are imagining the taste of a juicy steak all while you are still reading the Bible, you ask yourself, "What have I just read?" As mentioned earlier, praying before reading gives you a clear mind of understanding which will keep you focused especially when you begin reading the Bible, try it.

PUTTING IT ALL IN CONTENT

One thing I have found with the many translations of the Bible on hand is that after reading a whole chapter of one version of the

Bible and coming up with my own conclusions of what that chapter was saying was a major mistake. Many times after reading just one version, I would realize that I was way off base of understanding it.

Reading different versions or translations of the Bible can sometimes have me look at things from a different perspective or actually it would turn out to mean something totally different than what I initially thought it meant.

I've trained myself so that after reading a verse or two to go back and read it again to make sure that I understood it completely before reading more. Believe me though, it does not hurt to read the entire chapter to get a full understanding of it. It just took me a little longer to get to that point of reading the whole chapter all together.

When you get to the point to where reading scriptures is becoming enjoyable to you, you will find that it starts to sound like someone you personally know is speaking to you, well it is. Reading the Bible should be exciting and not a challenge or difficult to read.

Reflection and Relevant Questions

1. In this chapter, Paul talks about Obedience and Sacrifice.
   a. How can you relate those two words in your own life whereby you had to apply both in order to stay in alignment with parents, boss and with God? Explain.
   b. The Bible says that "Pride goeth before destruction, and an haughty spirit before a fall" (Proverbs 16:18 KJV). Name a time in your life when your selfish pride got in the way and stopped you from doing what was right or beneficial and caused a negative result.

2. Read James 5:13--18 where it talks about the power in prayers. Praying is a very important aspect in our daily lives today. It is our communication with God. How important is praying meant in your daily life?
   a. What do you expect out of your prayers and when do you know that your prayers have been heard and fulfilled?
   b. What are some portions of the Bible you have found difficult? List them and ask the Holy Spirit to guide you into a better understanding of those scriptures.

3. Do you feel disappointed when your prayers are not answered immediately or in a timely manner? Why
   a. Can you sincerely and honestly pray for people who are treating you poorly? Explain

4

>>»»»»» «««««««

MAKE A STAND

"Come to me, all ye that labour and are heavy
laden, and I will give you rest. Take my yoke upon
you, and lean on me; for I am meek and lowly in
heart: and ye shall find rest unto your souls."
(Matthew 11:28-29 KJV)

ave you ever felt so weak or torn down and you feel like you are a total mess and that God cannot use you? Your body and mind has been through so much hurt and pain and you have gotten to the point to where you have thrown up your hands and are saying to others and to yourself, "You know what, I just give up!" Hold on! There is Great news, you are in the perfect position and you are ready to be used by God to be a vessel!

Years ago, after suffering from a major coma, I felt totally useless. My memory was gone, not being able to walk, not to mention the thought of never writing again, yeah I was at one of my lowest points in my life, But even then God was using me during that period of my life.

God had me in the perfect position He wanted me to be in. Even though at times I felt like I was having a nervous breakdown, my situation of being bed ridden, my situation with finances, my situation of being useless actually brought family and loved ones back together again and I did not have to do anything.

Purpose will tell you to stand when your pride is telling you to give up. Believe me, you are never too broken for God!

THE BREAKDOWN OF THE FAMILY

One of the first things God created was the family when He created man and women. It was the hopes of God that man and women would multiply and fill the earth with people who would fulfil His purpose but, somewhere along the way, things got off track.

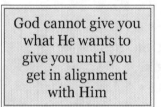

God cannot give you what He wants to give you until you get in alignment with Him

In order for God's purpose to be fulfilled and the family to survive, each person in the family has a part to play. This is not only beneficial to the family but is important to our society as a whole. It all starts with having a strong family background. Think about it like this:

Strong Families, build strong Communities,
Strong communities, build strong Cities,
Strong cities will build strong States,
Strong states will build a strong Country!

There is authority in the household-namely, the parents. Every household has a vision. I do not believe that men and women can do whatever or be whomever they feel like they can be in the family household. I truly believe that God had established roles in the family. It all starts with the family structure and who is the head of the family, actually Christ is, then comes the man, then comes the woman and then the children. When the head is in the right place of alignment, the anointing will flow down to the rest of the family and the enemy will know that something great is about to happen in your life but, God cannot give you what He wants to give you until you get in right alignment. Have we lost that alignment perspective or family order?

MEN, IT'S TIME TO TAKE
YOUR RIGHTFUL PLACE!

Now, please understand something. Being a man, I can only speak from the perspective of a man, ok? When my children were younger during the first several years of my wife and I being married, we brought our first brand new home. We were very happy to actually hold the deed in our hands which proudly displayed both of our names. After some time, we started receiving letters regarding various taxes affiliated with owning a new home which some came in my wife's name and some came in my name.

But when the actual tax bill finally arrived in our mailbox it only came in my name. Why was that? Was it because of the way we filled out the forms? Was it because I was the one mostly talking to them over the phone? Or could it be that me being a man of the house they assumed that I was the head of the household which I was, because I am the Man! (*Don't tell my wife I said that ok?*)

Whatever the case was, I have to admit that it is rather rewarding by being a man but I have to tell you that it comes with a lot of responsibilities. Even though both of our names were on the deed, when the time came for payment of the taxes, they sought me out because I was overall responsible.

If either one of those tax bills were not paid and we would had lost anything especially the house, everything would have fallen on me because me being the man of the house I was overall responsible for making sure the family had proper shelter, providing food and security, God created us that way. The Bible says this regarding the Husband and the Man of the house:

1. He should love God more than anyone or anything. God is to be his top priority above everyone this includes his wife (Ephesians 5:22-25).
2. He should be a leader and a provider for the family whether it be physically, financially, or spiritually. "But if any provide not for his own, and especially for those of his own house, he

hath denied the faith, and is worse than an infidel"(1Timothy 5:8 KJV).

3. He should be courageous meaning that your fear of God is greater than that of men.
4. He should love his wife and not be ashamed to show his love for her publicly and openly.

OK men let's agree, God did not create a woman to be the head of the household, He did not create the women to be the sole provider for the family, He created a woman to be a helper to us men. But, somewhere throughout time, somewhere along the lines the roles have gotten mixed up or reversed.

> "Husbands love you wives, even as Christ also loved the church, and gave Himself for it"(Eph. 5:25kjv)

We are living in a society where a father's worth is almost lost and if you look at men today period, the value of a man has slowly been devalued. Most men have been marked by their Fathers and have taken on many of their traits some good and some bad, but still again, Fathers are the most important person in the household.

There are special things that you can only get from a father. Actually, I can remember the first time my Daddy said, "Junior, I love you, I am proud of you." Many people have said those words to me but when it came from my Daddy, it hit me in a certain place, it got emotional and it stopped me in my tracks.

Why is it that when certain words coming from a father seem to be a little bit more special than usual? Now, I am not taking anything away from our mothers at all, but at this point I am referring specifically about the fathers.

It does not matter if your father was a good one or a terrible one, locked up, homeless, or could care less about the family, when your father speak certain words to you, it hits home and causes you to stop and think for a moment.

Now, there is nothing wrong with being financially successful especially if your success is the result of God blessing you on your honest efforts, but at the same time, while fathers are working hard building a life financially(*increasing bank account*), building a physical life(*buying cars, big houses etc.)* for the family many are forgetting all about building and valuing what is most important to the family: *Creating future Vessels.*

How are you going to be a vessel of honor for Christ within the family and not raising your children to be Vessels? Men, you are not raising kids, you are raising men and women. Believe me, the little ones are listening to what you say but more importantly, they are following what you do!

You hear your child saying words they have no clue as to what it means or crossing their knees in a certain way while sitting, you see them sipping on something out of a cup with the pinky finger sticking up a certain way, of course they have been watching you and listening to you, just watch them, they are a reflection of you! At the same time they also want to learn about God!

> Men, you are not raising kids, you are raising men and women.

Every man should be building a family of vessels. A family that matters where a boy can grow to become a man and where a girl can grow to become a woman. Believe me when I say that they will not be children for long, they grow up fast. You are a reflection of God's handy work, your spouse should complete you and represent the fullness of you and your children are a direct reflection of you.

It is sad to say that so many women are taking on roles that they were not equipped nor designed to do. I will give you a few examples. Roles such as leading the family spiritually, providing shelter and basically being head of the household remember, (*that's the man's job*). Still again we continue putting the blame on the woman for everything that has ever negatively happened within the family structure.

Men, let me ask you a question. First off, surely you remember the story of Adam and Eve, right? Yeah we all do. They were both allowed to enjoy everything in the garden but were told not to eat from the tree of knowledge.

Remember, it was the disobedience of Eve who the serpent deceived into eating the forbitten fruit but, this was not the first time Eve had seen the Tree of Knowledge but it was the first time that she had actually seen it through the eyes of Satin which makes the difference. That is exactly what Satin wants for you and I, to see things through his eyes and not God's.

It was Eve who got Adam to also take a bite out of the forebitten fruit, right? Eve chose to eat the forbitten fruit thus destroying their innocence, purity and eventually bringing death into their lives, right? After the forbitten fruit was eaten and their eyes were now opened they all got a severe punishment from God, including the serpent.

God punished the serpent for enticing Eve into eating the forbitten fruit:

"Because thou hast done this, thou art cursed above all cattle, upon thy belly shalt thou go" (Genesis 3:14 KJV).

God punished Eve for eating the forbitten fruit:

"Unto the woman He said, I will greatly multiply thy sorrow and thy conception; in sorrow thou shalt bring forth children; and thy desire shall be to thy husband, and he shall rule over thee" (Genesis 3:16 KJV).

And God punished Adam not so much that he ate the forbitten fruit but more importantly because he chose to listen to Eve instead of listening to God:

"Because thou hast harkened unto the voice of thy wife and hast eaten of the tree, of which I commanded thee, saying, Thou shalt not eat of it: cursed is the ground for thy sake; in sorrow shalt thou eat of it all the days of thy life;"

(Genesis 3:17 KJV).

Adam only had one job to do, "To dress and keep the garden of Eden"(Genesis 2:15 kjv).

Now think about something, If Adam would had followed those few simple instructions this whole story may have taken a totally different turn.

God asked Adam one simple question:

"Where are thou?" (Genesis 3:9 kjv)

He did not ask Eve anything, not yet anyway. He questioned Adam because he was created to be the head of the family to look after Eve and to take care of the garden, right?

If you remember reading the scripture, the serpent gave Eve the forbitten apple to eat and she ate it? But guess what, Adam was standing right beside her when this was all taking place and he did absolutely nothing to stop the serpent from enticing Eve nor did he stop her from eating it.

"And when the women saw that the tree was good for food, and that it was pleasant to the eyes, and a tree to be desired to make one wise, she took of the fruit thereof, and did eat, and gave also unto <u>her husband with her</u>, and he did eat" (Genesis 3:6 KJV).

Yes, Adam was standing right there next to Eve while she ate the forbitten fruit, now who was to blame? I still say Adam, I blame Adam because he was not on his P's and Q's. Think about something. God put Adam over the Garden of Eden meaning that he was "to dress and keep it." From a spiritual aspect, God's primary plan for Adam "to dress and keep it" was to worship Him and to observe what He tells Him.

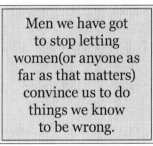

Men we have got to stop letting women(or anyone as far as that matters) convince us to do things we know to be wrong.

From a physical aspect, "to dress and keep it" means to cultivate and protect the garden of Eden. Now, if Adam was there to protect the garden then the serpent would never had been allowed entry in the garden to deceive Eve.

But, at the same time, if Eve would have been on her P's and Q's, she would stopped the serpent in his tracks and told him, "You can't give me what I already have, did you forget that I was fearfully and marvelously made in the image of God, what else can you possibly offer me that I don't already have?" But that was not the case.

Eve was put in a position where she had no clue of the instructions given by God to Adam regarding what was good or bad in the garden and was left to make her own decisions. That's what happens when we as men take a back seat and don't stand up for our family. Anyway Adam should have been listening to the voice of God instead of Eve whispering in his ear(*Men we have got to stop letting women(or anyone as far as that matters) convince us to do things we know to be wrong*). Actually, Adam even tried to blame the entire incident on poor Eve. Can't you hear Adam trying to plead his case to God:

> "Hast thou eaten of the tree, whereof I commanded thee that thou shouldest not eat?" And the man said, "The woman whom thou gavest to be with me, she gave me of the tree, and I did eat" (Genesis 3:11-12 KJV).

> It is one thing when a young man don't have a father figure present but when there is no spiritual father in his life, he is without a father twice.

Yep, ole Adam was not trying to take the blame for anything. But I blame Adam for the fall because first, he was the head of the family and did not do his job. Secondly, Adam did not protect the garden nor did he protect Eve.

Yeah, Adam was there throughout the whole thing even while she was being tricked into eating the apple and he did nothing, do you see a problem with that?

SET YOUR HOUSE IN ORDER

It is crazy that men are very present today and will even be in the same house day and night, eating with the family and still not be present because they are silent and not fulfilling their roles God has created or designed them to do!

We men will sit on the couch and play on the play station hours at a time while our wives will be washing dishes, folding clothes, cutting the lawn and so on.

We expect our wives to be Joan Cleaver during the day and a playmate at night, I'm telling you, it's not going to work. Believe me fellas, I would rather be playing with my wife than be playing on a play station any day or night, it's much more fun!

Worse than that, while you are attending church praising and worshipping God, your children are home playing on your play station. Put some clothes on those kids and take them with you to church for a change.

Think about even this, "Is it right for you to spend more time golfing or fishing over that of teaching your child about the Bible and about God?" If your child was asked to say a dinner prayer or recite a Bible verse, would they be able to do it? Children/teenager needs discipline and believe it or not, they want to be disciplined, it's a part of them. They will respect and love you more for providing discipline and at the same time lose respect towards you for not.

Besides, how can you expect your child to one day become a vessel to be used by Christ if you are not initially setting the example? It is one thing when a young man don't have a father figure present but when there is no spiritual father in his life, he is without a father twice. As mentioned earlier, our children are the direct reflection of the parents and it starts with the Head of the household, You!

There comes a time in life when we must decide to grow up. I know you are grown but sometimes we may have an adult body, an adult age and even a great job and still be having the mindset of a child. It does not matter what condition the family is in, it can be resolved.

> Women were created to be a helper to the man, not your main means of support

Listen my brothers, you may have major differences with the one you once loved but, I'm here to tell you that you two can be reconciled in one way or another through the blood of Christ Jesus. If not done for yourselves, then do it for the children they deserve it, don't you agree?

If you think for one single moment that a woman enjoys or prefers to be head of the house, I suggest you think twice. Women were created to be a helper to the man, not your main means of support. That is why Eve was created, to complete Adam. But, in all actuality, we have left our females no other choice but to step in the role of heading and leading everything, even when it comes to the church, all you have to do is look around the Sunday morning audience and you will see who the majority is. I ask you again my dear brothers in Christ:

"Where are you?"

We have to decide what is most important when it comes to the family. We are the head of the house hold. Our job description includes: Spiritual leadership, providing shelter, security and so on. It is a big job, but God has equipped and prepared you for it.

It is time for all men to stand up and step into our position and utilize the God given authority He has ordained for you and I! It is time to take control over Satan's plan before he takes control over your family and you need to proclaim like Joshua did: "BUT AS FOR ME AND MY HOUSE, WE WILL SERVE THE LORD!" (Joshua 24:15 kjv)

WOMEN, IT'S TIME TO TAKE YOUR RIGHTFUL PLACE!

Like a lot of men, I love watching college football games. There are times after the big game is over, the star players are sometimes asked to give a short television interview regarding the outcome. I remember watching one college game interview in particular.

Before the interviewer could start, the star football player grabbed the mike and the first words to come out of his mouth was, "I would like to give a big shout out to my Mom, hi Mom I love you."

Now there was absolutely nothing wrong with him saying that unless you were his father. That same father who taught the son the game, that same father who trained and was at every game that son played in, that same father who tossed the football with him and taught him the fundamentals of the game.

Through high school and even after entering college that same father was still present at every game pushing and keeping him in shape, encouraging and still working hard to keep him on track.

But that same son after scoring his first winning touchdown while the Dad is in the stands cheering him on and the mother is home smiling ironing clothes, during a national televised interview, the first words to come out that same son's mouth is,

"I would like to thank and give a huge shout out
to my Mom, hi Mom, I love you." Why was that?

It was because even though the Dad provided encouragement and physical training, it was the mother who provided physical nourishment, safety, love and emotional comfort.

> Our mothers were always the one who you could run to after falling to the ground hurting yourself, the one who always had a comforting hug even after you had gotten a spanking

Our mothers were always the one who you could run to after falling to the ground hurting yourself, the one who always had a comforting hug even after you had gotten a spanking. A mother is special and do not always have to say things like, "I'm proud of you" or "Good job" just her smile gave confidence and reassurance that everything was fine and for you to keep doing what you are doing.

I think that I have been rather hard on the fathers and the men. Now I want to speak to the mothers and the woman of the family for a moment. God created the women to be the fullness and a helper to the man and to provide nourishment to the family but somewhere throughout time that role has slowly diminished or worse, reversed.

All throughout the Bible, it shows where women did evil against their husbands or were even disobedient to God. Take for example the woman we talked about a little earlier, Eve. Eve had the perfect life. She had the ideal man in her life, she did not have to worry about controlling her weight, she did not have to worry about cooking and cleaning. Eve did not even have to worry about the pain associated with child birth, at least not yet.

And like I mentioned before, even having this so-called perfect life it was still not enough for Eve, she wanted more than what God was providing for them. After the incident in the garden, God asked Eve one simple question:

"What is this that thou hast done?"(Gen. 3:13 kjv)

Eve made three mistakes. First, she listened to the serpent, secondly, she ate the forbitten fruit then thirdly, she gave a bite to Adam and in their disobedience *they* no longer had the perfect lifestyle of the rich and famous life (Genesis 3:1-16 kjv). Don't let the things around you destroy what's inside of you.

OK, what about Job's wife? It's probably a good thing that her name was never mentioned so we will continue to simply call her "Job's wife." After losing his health wealth and children(Job 1:13-22 kjv), while she and Job were experiencing perhaps the worst times of their life, she gave Job the worst advice ever to man, "Curse God and die" and that was exactly what Satan wanted Job to do(Job 2:9 kjv).

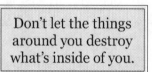

Don't let the things around you destroy what's inside of you.

Satan was not after Job's wife, he never had no intentions of ever having any contact or dealings with her. Satin was after Job thinking that if he could get to the head honcho, if he could destroy the head of the family then the rest of the family did not have a fighting chance of survival. Satan's goal is to deny your destiny by distracting you from God. This was just another attempt to prove Satins point that if all was taken away from Job he would turn his back on God. It was only after all else had failed that Satin used Job's wife to get to Job and still Satins attempts did not work.

Over time women have either chosen to take a step back and decided not to help at all or took a step forward wanting to be the head of the household even when the man is present. This can become confusing and cause many arguments especially when the man of the house is trying to do his job.

The family requires unity and unity requires submission. Just like man summits to God, the children submits to the parents, the wife is supposed to represent the fullness of the husband and submit to him, that's in the Bible (Ephesians 5:22 kjv).

There has to be structure in the family in order for it to survive. Children want and need structure in the family more than anyone else and when one person tries to step into another person's shoes, the whole household gets out of alignment and things becomes confusingly unbalanced. The man should not take a backseat and let the women be the head and the woman should not be trying to be the head. And

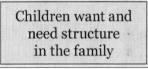

Children want and need structure in the family

above all things, the children for sure should not be telling or advising the parents on how the house should be ran, simple as that.

Yes, men were created to be the head of the family household and at times things can become very difficult for them but believe me when I say that we still need that soft voice of reassurance from the wife to help us make it along the way.

A man can have all the riches in the world and be wanting for nothing but, it will mean nothing if he has no one to share it with.

Mothers/Wives we need you

A women can either be a voice of comfort or one that is always angry with never a positive word to say. Many men put on the facade as being strong and can handle anything and everything that comes our way but inside many of us are confused and at times afraid of failing the family but because of pride can't and will refuse to let that side of us show.

The children need mothers to be at their beck and call and at the same time provide that special hug as only they can give, well men need the same things too.

I have three daughters and I would often say to them "Daughters cling to their Fathers and Sons cling to their Mothers." Over the years I have come to realize that not to be so true. I have learned that daughters and sons cling to their mothers and yes, husbands indeed cling to their wives as well!

Mothers, you play an important part in the family structure but, we need you to step up your game. Especially if you are in the position of being the head of the household, your job has become that more challenging. Children have their own demons to face each day, ones you may not even be aware of or paying attention to. Many of them face bullies on a daily basis, many deal with depression, loneliness and some may even feel that they don't even have a place in the family. You as a single parent have to fill the gap and keep assuring them what family is all about. Remember you are not raising a son or daughter, you are raising men and women!

> Remember, you are not raising a son or daughter, you are raising men and women!

I understand the fact that through no result of your own as to why you have had no other choice but to step into the role of being both parents the father and the mother but I'm here to tell you that as hard as you may try, there are things that can only come from the father of that child.

You can try to keep the children from their father's from seeing each other, but in the long run, there will be a missing whole in their hearts, both the father and the child. You can be the connecting gap to making the ones in the family feel like they are a family. No matter how terrible the parents are, a child's biggest wish is for the family to be together for a lifetime.

CHILDREN, IT'S TIME TO TAKE YOUR RIGHTFUL PLACE

Now, when it comes to the children's and even the teens role or position in the family, this should be an easy one especially for the father and the mother to figure out because it was not too long ago to where we held those same positions. You might ask, "What do you mean an easy one for the father and the mother?" I know that parenting is not easy and does not come with a manual or instructions but where are the children and teens going to know their role or their place in the family if at least not one of the parent's don't or didn't instruct them?

When I was younger, especially my mother would often say things to me like, "Mind your business Junior"

or "Don't get too big for your britches boy" and I would often think to myself, "What are britches?" I didn't know what britches were at the time, but by the tone of her voice, I did know that there were going to be consequences and repercussions if I kept doing what I was doing.

A child's role in the family is simply this: to be a child seen and not heard, nothing else. Not the financial provider(child support) and most definitely not to be the parent of the house over you. A child has to be a child and they are constantly listening and learning. Perhaps you didn't notice your child sitting around and listening and even involving

> A child's role in the family is simply this: to be a child seen and not heard nothing else

themselves in adult conversations. Perhaps you have failed to observe who your child's friends are.

So you can't blame them when they start to talk back to adults or start smoking at a young age because either you have allowed the behavior or they could have gotten the habit from you and figured it to be ok. Children are going to learn one way or another, good information or bad they are going to learn.

God has preprogrammed our minds and we all learn in different ways but think about how a child/teen learns. A child/teen learns in three ways:

1. **From <u>Auditory</u>**: When a baby is first born they do a lot of listening for example from hearing soft songs sung by the mother, to the talks of advice you give them as a preteen/ teenager. Have you ever notice one of your young ones

43

repeating back something that you had said to them before? Believe me, they are listening to you.

2. **From <u>Watching</u>**: When I was growing up, the best video game on the market was the Atari where we played ping pong on a black and white screen. If you had one of those gaming systems, you were the talk of the town.

Recently, I moved up my game and I brought a Pac-man game to play on my television. One of my grandsons came to visit recently and proudly I allowed him to play on it. Within fifteen minutes he was asking, "Do you have anything else we can play with besides this?" He had gotten bored that quick.

Probably the one thing especially our teens are exposed to and corrupting our children today is the internet. Even my grandchildren have tablets where they can surf the internet for games and even communicate with friends across the world instantly.

I thought to myself, if they have so much access to surf the internet to help with homework, play games and to communicate with friends, what else do they have access to, pornography, sex and recently this thing called Tic-Tok.

While we are thinking that they are playing innocent and harmless games on the internet, you really have to ask yourself, "What are our children really watching and learning from all this access?" I tell you that the worse thing for a child is to learn and get educated in the wrong direction.

There was a song we used to sing in Sunday school which went a little like this: Be careful little eyes what you see, Be careful little eyes what you see, for the father up above is looking down on us, be careful little eyes what you see."

> Train up a child in the way he should go: and when he is old, he will not depart from it.
> Proverbs 22:6 KJV

Children learn from watching especially from us. It is your responsibility as a parent to supervise and to teach the children what is appropriate and what is not. Not just on the internet but in life in general itself.

As a child/teenager, it is your responsibility to obey your parents and to follow Godly advice from them. The Bible says:

"Children, obey your parents in the Lord: for this is right. Honour thy father and mother; which is the first commandment with promise; That it may be well with thee, and thou mayest live long on the earth" (Ephesians 6:1-3 KJV).

It did not say to obey them if they were good parents or bad parents, the scripture simply says "Children, obey your parents" that's all(Ephesians 6:1 kjv),. So parents be careful what they are watching, especially when they are watching you.

3. **From Experience**: Most of a child's learning come from simple trial and error. They touch something that is too hot, they will not touch it again. They do something good they will get rewarded and at the same time if they do something wrong and gets punished for it more than likely they won't do it again. All this comes during the learning stages.

But, do not get me wrong, there comes a time in a child's life when they must decide to put away childish things and begin to grow up and start to show some maturity in themselves. Sometimes no matter how much you say to them, no matter how many times you show a child something, the only way they can fully catch on whether they fail or succeed at it is to allow them to try it for themselves, hands on.

While homeschooling our three daughters my wife and I realized that the three of them learned in three totally different ways.

One child learned from reading the material, one child learned from me telling her about the material first and the other daughter learned from actual hands on with the material we were discussing.

Either way of learning was very effective but the approach was different for each and we had to put together a curriculum designed specifically for each individual child.

In all actuality, even we as a young adults or as a grown up still learn and receive things in the same manner in which we were taught. But as we have matured we can look back and see how God kept us in line, how our life was all designed by Him and that our life is lived in stages.

Yes, there may have been some difficult days throughout your lifetime but you can sincerely see how things were done in stages and in order but you made it through. Just look at a few of God's people who had to go through various stages of life and came through:

Think about <u>Joseph</u>:

1. He was favored but despised by brothers.
2. He was sold into slavery.
3. Brought by Potiphar one of Pharaohs Guardsmen.
4. He rose to become second in command in Egypt next to Pharaoh.

<u>Think about Esther:</u>

1. She was an orphan raised by Mordecai.
2. She was chosen to be Queen of Persia.
3. She helped to save the Jewish nation.

<u>Think about Moses:</u>

1. He survived a killing of all the male babies
2. He was rescued by Pharoah's daughter
3. He Led the people of Israel through the Red Sea.

We all live in stages but regarding the children, it is time for them to take their rightful place that of being a child but it is our responsibility to guide them in the right direction.

CHURCH, IT'S TIME TO TAKE YOUR RIGHTFUL PLACE!

The Bible warns us that there will be days when right will be called wrong and wrong will be declared right. Over the past decade, the church has become so worldly and the world has tried to seem so churchy to the point that many times you can't even tell the difference between the two. We have seen some dramatic changes throughout our society to where a man and a woman is not even considered to be a normal marriage, to where a person's gender is not even relevant or important anymore. But what's more interesting is that a lot of these changes that occurred within our society started right there, within the church.

When the church begins to accept things like Pastors misleading entire congregations and nothing is being said or done about it, churches being more concerned with filling bank accounts as opposed to filling souls, it effects our society as a whole.

It all starts with a division within the body of the church. Leaders being more concerned with personal recognition rather than saving souls, leaders being more concerned with achieving bigger and higher titles and status within those same four walls rather than serving the community. Even within our local churches you can see where yes believers are becoming more outspoken

> The biggest issue churches are dealing with today is "Division"

but are settling and accepting less than what is required by God and have even forgotten what is normal. You find believers coming to church expecting to be entertained rather than hearing a word from the Lord. Members thinking they can do a better job than someone else even a better job than the Pastor. When you find certain members causing havoc, members fighting and disagreeing among themselves within the church, the Anointing of the Holy Spirit cannot and will come in.

The Bible speaks of two things, repentance and a great falling away of the church. That being said, I still think that one of the biggest issues that churches are dealing with today is Division: Division occurs when you are sizing up someone based on skin color, income, where they live, their gender and all kinds of crazy odd things. Churches are divided when it comes to money, churches are divided on how the choir should sing or songs to be sung, they are even divided on the way communion is to be given. Communion is supposed to bring us together not only with God but also with each other. What exactly are we looking for in a church? One thing for sure though, if you are looking for the perfect church here on earth, you are not going to find it. Every church has its good points and some not so desired ones. The only perfect church will only be found in Heaven.

God is not looking for a better singing choir, He is not concerned on the way you serve communion(*because it is explained in the Bible*), He is not looking for another church building and most definitely not looking for more pastors, God is looking for Disciples who are Vesseled and Prepared for the Kingdom!

Let's mend the division within the church because the devil knows that if he can break-up the unity, he can break-up the church and that God will not operate when the church is divided therefore effecting the kingdom. Let's get back in alignment and get back to the basics, we need unity! There is power in unity! God calls us into unity:

> "That they may be one; as thou, Father, art in me, and I in thee, that they may also be one in us: that the world may believe that thou hast sent me" (John 17:21 KJV).

Unity says that we are in line and followers of Jesus Christ. Within the church we all have different talents but unity will bring us together. But still again, people and I mean good people are being disqualified because they can't sing like you, they are disqualified because they don't know the Bible as well as you do.

We disqualify people because we want them to be what we want them to be and to be where we are. Don't disqualify someone based on their level of experience or their ability and quit comparing yourself to others, just be yourself.

We are all different and called for different reasons. Some people are called to go out to all the nations seeking and serving lost souls and some are called to go home to their spouse. We are all different but we are still part of one body. You don't ask the foot to do what the hand can do but working together the body works.

When visiting the city of Corinth, Apostle Paul wrote to God's beloved people in Rome: *"And we know that all things work together for good to them that love God, to them who are Called according to his Purpose"*(Rom 8:28 kjv).

You don't ask the accountant to do what the choir director does in the church but working together the church works. Each has their own talent and when you put them all together, unity develops.

I once heard that when an ancient king captured a prisoner, he would cut off their thumb and their big toe. That way the prisoner could no longer hold a sword nor hold their balance while standing. The prisoner was not killed simply because he was no longer a threat.

You may consider yourself to be the least among many like the thumb and the toe, but without either of these the body would suffer.

Without you, your talents and gifts being cut off, the church will be stagnated and will suffer, either we all go together or we don't go at all, remember that. The bottom line is that we all are in need of repentance. Think about it:

What was the first command Jesus preached? *Repentance.*

What was the message John the Baptist preached? *Repentance.*

Repentance is the easy part, unity is the hard part. Let us cry out:

"LORD HELP US TO BE UNIFIED AGAIN!"

STOP WATERING IT DOWN!

Over the years many churches have lost focus on what is most important and that is "Preparing lost souls for the coming of Christ"

49

and slowly have moved from that doctrine to focusing more on attendance and tithes. Of course it takes money to run a church but

> "Therefore Come out from among them and be separate, says the Lord. Do not touch what is unclean, and I will receive you" (2 Cor (2:17 kjv)

is it possible to apply our focus on preparing lost souls for the coming of Christ and at the same time keeping the attendance up?

We all so often wonder why one week there are two hundred believers in attendance and the following three weeks the attendance dropped to less than half of that. There used to be a time when the walls of the church would seemed to shake rattle and roll when the prayer warriors would cry out praising and worshipping but now, there seems to be a little more than silence during that time.

Jesus speaks about a church that is neither on fire nor is it cold but is rather luke warm. He's referring to the church at Laodicea(Rev. 3:14-17 kjv). Now from a physical point of view, you have to look at the churches location. On one side of the church of Laodicea was the city of Acropolis known for its hot springs and on the other side lied the city of Colossae where cold waters flowed down from the mountains. When the hot waters from the springs flowed into Laodicea and met the cold waters flowing down from the mountains of Colossae-you see where I'm going with this? But from a spiritual point of view, the city of Laodicea was criticized for their lack of zeal and their selfish focus on wealth which kept them living and fulfilling the purpose God set for their lives. They felt that with their wealth they had no need for anything else. Jesus therefore deemed the church-luke warm.

Today, Sunday messages have become luke warm so not to offend anyone and more importantly churches feel the need to keep them coming not to lose membership and if you are one those who are sitting there listening to these messages and you know you are living in sin, you are wrong and they are wrong, the church will receive judgement and you need to run!

"For the time is come that judgement must begin at the church of God: and if it first begin with us, what shall the end be of them that obey not the gospel of God?" (1Peter 4:17 KJV)

Week after week many dedicated believers will attend church, faithfully pay tithes and will support the church to the fullest extent any way they can. Things look like God and sounds like God but in reality it is not God. Slowly over time the enemy begins to step in and the plush green grass that once flourished throughout the church slowly starts turning brown.

The anointing that once flowed freely has dissipated and this not only applies to the Pastors and the leaders but this also applies to the entire body of the church which have become so numb and tolerant to hearing basic teachings that they think "That's all there is to it", but it's not.

> We are all in need of repentance

There comes a time in everyone's life when even the leaders will begin to mature wanting and seeking more of what God has to offer especially when it comes to the usual feel good luke warm messages, people want more, people want the fire of the Holy Ghost experience!

Jesus said, "I am the vine, you are the branches." We have to get to a place where we can get back connected to the vine, Jesus!

With everything that is going on in the world today people's eyes and ears are opening up and they are beginning to realize more and more Bible prophecies quickly coming to pass leaving them wanting a higher understanding of it all.

People are tired of the same ole feel-good watered-down messages week after week. People are getting excited, people's hearts are being stirred up and more than ever they are seeking new meat or in other words a deeper teaching of the gospel.

While churches are not teaching holiness and the deeper truths, people are crying out for the rains of heaven to fall down upon their soul, they are desperate for the anointed fires from God to come upon them like never before and if they can't cry out to the lord in the

House of God then what exactly is the church really doing for them? It's time for a change!

> "For the time is coming when people will not endure sound teaching, but having itching ears they will accumulate for themselves teachers to suit their own passions" (2 Timothy 4:3 esv).

Think about it like this, when it came time to raising your children and they would come to you for sound advice, you did not waver in telling and giving them the best advice you could and the absolute truth. You did not give half advice or try to tell them something to make them feel good you laid it all out on the table.

Would you take advice on marriage from someone who has been divorced three times? Would you take advanced math calculus tutoring lessons from someone who failed eighth grade math? No!

Then why is it any different when it comes to the teachings of the gospel? Why are we listening to half-truths or worse teaching watered down half-truths of the gospel just to please ears? Why are we feeding believers candy when they are hungry wanting the full buffet, meat, sides, salad, drinks and all? Churches are having church, but not having an encounter.

We have to get back in alignment with the Word of God and start ministering and teaching the whole truth and nothing but the truth even if it is hurtful to some. And when the church begins to start teaching how to deal with Satin when he is destroying their family, when the church begin to teach how Jesus was raised from the dead, when churches begin to teach how

> God has called His people to be Vessels of Honor and the only way that can be done is to mature.

one can not only make it to the gates of heaven but how they can actually make it inside the gates of heaven and live a glorious life with the Father, you won't have to worry about attendance or how much tithes were received after the service, the church will be able to take care of itself!

Believe me when I say that you will not lose one member when you begin to start teaching on:

*   The Second coming of Christ
*   Being filled and walking in Holiness
*   The Mysteries of the Word of God

When the church begin to start teaching the true biblical gospel, yes, some feelings may get hurt and you may lose members but it will only be for a season. God will send new members, ones who are faithful, ones who are willing to work and have a sincere desire in carrying out the churches goals and fulfilling God's overall design for the church!

Jesus told Peter, "I will build my church and the gates of hell shall not prevail" (Matthew 16:18 KJV) but this is going to require the church to start advancing to a higher spiritual level. The Bible says to bring your gifts to the alter but, we find churches saying "Leave that at home." Prophesying and speaking in tongues, "Ah, could you do that at home," dancing shouting praising God out loud, "Ah, could you keep it at a minimum." Getting filled with the Holy Ghost, but you will have to be taken out of the sanctuary. What do you think about that?

Each week churches are asking for you to come and will welcome you with open arms, but they don't want your manifestation and surly they don't want your fire. They want folks to get healed and the church will cry out, "Come Lord Come" but at the same time muting and quenching the Holy Spirit.

A lot of churches don't want change simply because when peoples gifts are being displayed, prophecies coming forth and the fire of the Holy Ghost enters, it stirs people up and many people become afraid and don't understand especially new believers and they will choose to leave never experiencing God's glory. I ask you, "How can God be glorified when peoples gifts are being quenched and are not being allowed in the church?" Yes, believers who are on fire for God can still use a little bit more of the Holy Ghost fire!

"Father, we need You more than ever right now! Please send down your manifested glory and fill our hearts, minds and soul with Your presence. Let the fire of the Holy Ghost engulf our heart, let Your presence surround our poor souls. We want that experience with You Lord like never before, I am thirsty for You Lord, please hear my cry oh Lord, amen."

Believe me, no matter what, God will be glorified and has called His people to be Vessels of Honor but the only way that can be done is to allow your Spiritual gift to mature.

Just like a plant, in order for it to grow it requires nourishment from the soil and a lot of patience before it matures. In order for people to mature they need growth. In order for a person to grow, they need patience and nourishment from one teaching them before they can mature. More than anything else, they need the power of the Holy Spirit that will convict, convince and convert them.

In the book of Matthew Jesus gave His disciples one commission and that was to:

> "Go ye therefore, and teach all nations, baptizing them in the name of the Father, and the Son, and of the Holy Ghost: Teaching them to observe all things whatsoever I have commanded you: and, lo, I am with you always, even unto the end of the world, Amen"(Matthew 28:19-20 KJV).

How is anyone going to be a vessel for God and follow what it says in the book of Revelations, "You must prophesy again about many peoples, nations, languages and kings"(Rev. 10:11 kjv), how is anyone going to be able to go out and spread the true gospel if they are not being taught God's word with full understanding of it with nothing being held back?

> "Will you be the one to jumpstart God's Vessels to a higher level of deeper truths?"

So where do we start? How and when do we implement the deeper teachings of Christ within our assembly when we have been teaching feel good messages all along? My friend, there is no better time than now to start teaching and spreading God's word accordingly. Question is, "Will you be the one to jumpstart God's Vessels to a higher level of deeper truths?"

<u>Reflection and Relevant Questions</u>

1. In this chapter we talked about "Deny Compromising." Why is it so hard to resist compromising especially when it comes to our children, foods, even things we want but don't really need?

2. In this chapter Paul talks about Deeper Truths. Explain the difference between Traditional teachings and Deeper truths?

3. Indeed the church has changed in so many ways throughout time, but God has always stayed the same no matter what. In your local church, name some ways in which you have seen changes good or bad and list some ways you yourself can make a change for the betterment of the body.

5

>> >> >> >> >> >> << << << << << << <<

BE STILL

Be still and know that I am God. I will
be exalted among the nations, I will be
exalted in the earth. (Psalms 46 kjv)

any of Jesus disciples were harden fishermen but because of their location in the Sea of Galilee, (*which is actually a lake, the largest freshwater lake in the world*) the tides, the atmosphere and the waters were completely different. They were surrounded by mountains and hilltops which caused unusual violent windstorms unlike the ones they were familiar with.

The Latin word for Storm is *procella* meaning hurricane. There was a hurricane under the sea directly under their boat. Even though they were under the covering of God, they still found themselves in the midst of a terrible situation, in the middle of the sea in a massive hurricane. How much worse could things possibly be for them?

Many of us often times find ourselves in similar situations as the disciples were, where we desperately seek to remain under God's protective covering while still being in the midst of a terrible storm. You have to remember that just because you are a Christian it does not exempt you from the troubles of this world. Don't think that just because you go to church you are exempt from being attacked.

Jesus can be right there in the midst of your life and Satan can still try to interrupt your day. Think about what we just read when the disciples were faced with a storm, Jesus was there. Think about when Jesus walked with His twelve disciples, Judas was walking with Him.

Just because Jesus is in your life does not mean you are not going to deal some storms, but when you remain under God's covering, He will keep you.

The disciples panicked and were afraid of the storm and where was Jesus during the storm, He was sleeping comfortably resting on a cushion in the stern of the boat. The disciples were losing their minds out of fear from the storm and cried out to the Lord, "Master, carest thou not that we perish?" (Mark 4:38 KJV) Jesus arose and rebuked the wind, and said to the sea, "Peace be still" and there was a great calm (vs 39). The disciples then said one to another, "What manner of man is this, that even the wind and sea obey him?"(Mark 4:41 kjv) The disciple were afraid of the sea, but now they were terrified at what Jesus had just done. You can see here Jesus did not speak to the disciples, He spoke to the storm and it obeyed Him.

A thing about troubles and storms in our lives, they all share one thing in common: They both seem to occur during the most inconvenient, least expected worst times during our lifetime. What do you do when Jesus is in the midst of your family and the family is going through a storm? What do you do when Jesus is in the midst of your marriage and you are dealing with a storm? There are going to be times throughout your life when the doctors have failed you, medicines wearing off and you are going to have to speak to the storms crossing your path and just cry out, "Satin get thee behind me!"

We all need a sense of peace in our lives today. I guess after a long day of ministering to the multitude and to the disciples Jesus just needed a time to be alone on the boat, to relax and get away from it all and what better place especially during a terrible storm to find it other than under the stern of the boat, His personal breathing room.

Everyone needs a breathing room, a place to get away from it all. The place you think about going to after a hard day's work, after hours of sitting in a classroom or even spending sunup until sun down with two children both under the age of five, away from everyone and everything, from a world that seems to be running like an energized bunny. That breathing room is calling you to slow it down.

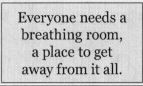

Everyone needs a breathing room, a place to get away from it all.

Two years ago, my wife and I visited a church in Chicago Illinois. Let me tell you that if you have ever driven on the mean highways of Atlanta Ga., New York city or Chicago then you already know what I am referring to when I say the "Fast Lane." The sign entering the highway advises a speed of 25mph, but the traffic on the highway is going 70mph. I entered the highways doing no less than 60mph!

Seems like everyone and everything always has to be done in a rush right now, and you just want to scream, "Peace Be Still"! Even food today has to be cooked in a rush. Believe it or not there used to be a time when it took over an hour to fully bake a potato, now you have instant potatoes. There used to be a time when it took a half an hour to make oatmeal, now you have instant oat meal ready in seconds.

I remember a time when you mailed off a letter, it could sometimes take weeks for the recipient to receive it. Now you can send a letter and the recipient can receive it instantly within seconds. We live in a world today where everything is expected to be done like I said, "Right now!"

You are never going to be placed in a situation where your faith can't get you out of!

The Bible says:

"Be still, and know that I am God"(Psalms 46:10 KJV).

Sometimes you are going to have to just be still for a moment. Take a step back and remember who is in charge. Yes, I know things need to get done and some in a timely manner but what is this rushing, panicking, gotta be done right now attitude doing to you physically, emotionally and spiritually?

Just like the disciples when they were terrified during the storm thinking they all were going to drown, Jesus asked them "Why are ye so fearful? How is it that ye have no faith?"(Mark 4:40 KJV) What happened to the, "I will be faithful till the end" attitude?

Before covid-19 hit everybody had faith, but when covid-19 hit, people's faith was tested. Should I get the shot or not? Should I wear a mask or not? People were even debating whether if they should go to church or not.

Have you lost faith that Jesus can handle anything? Just like He brought His disciples through the storm, He can and will bring you through your storms as well! Be still and remain faithful! You are never going to be placed in a situation where your faith can't get you out of.

Whatever storm you may be going through right now, whatever

God has a plan for your life!

battle you may be facing, you need to stop right now and give God some praise because He is about to bring you out! There have been times of betrayal, there have been times of disappointment, there were times you felt you could not make it, just keep

pressing and moving forward because He is about to bring you out into a new season in your life, His promises will come to pass! He will be with you even during the storm.

WHAT DO YOU WANT?

Friends and relatives alike want you to do what they want you to do by putting high expectations on you hoping that you will fulfill them but who is getting the benefits from it all, usually them. Parents want you to become what they want you to become. Even your employer wants you to act a certain way, speak a certain way especially when around other professionals, but what about you? Have you ever taken a moment and stepped back and asked yourself "What do I want to do in life or what do I expect out of life itself?"

When I finished high school, it seemed like my parents had a plan for me which is not a bad thing at all. We went to the library, looked over various professions, their respective salaries and so forth. After some time, the subject of accounting was decided to be my major, what I was to take up in college, my profession and basically what I would be doing the rest of my life. Sounds easy enough ha?

Well, only after one year of college, I knew that accounting was not for me, but God had a plan for me. I could not imagine working with numbers and figures all day but I continued in that field. After college, I worked a few minor jobs including entry level accounting work and to tell you the truth, I was miserable. As a matter of fact, sad to say, I had lost my own identity. It was several years before getting married that I actually asked myself the questions, "What do I really want out of life" and "Where do I see myself in five years?"

Have you ever pondered over the question, "What do I expect out of life?" Do you feel that your path has already been laid out and that there is nothing else left for you to accomplish?

It is true that God has an appointed time in your life for His purpose and plan to come to pass but that does not mean that you don't need to continue striving to be a better person or at least be the best at what you do.

If you are breathing and reading this then there is further work planned for you, life is not over!

You may mop floors for a living, so think positively and do your best and clean and shine those floors so that when people walk on them, they ask, "Who keeps these floors so shiny and clean?" You may cut grass for a living, so think positively and

> **Always striving to be a better person or striving to be the best at what you do!**

do your best by keeping the lawn cut so that it looks like a perfectly cut carpet.!

Think about this, the least likely skills you learned as a youth maybe you worked in a restaurant or a hat shop some of those skills can be useful even in your adult years. In my teen years I worked as a dishwasher and at times I was required to br*eakdow*n cardboard boxes to be placed in a dumpster. Believe it or not, I still today apply and use some of those same skills I learned as a teen such as being on time and how to treat people. Every opportunity to learn even the simplest things can be beneficial to you in some capacity or another.

Even now, you may be working at what you may consider to be a dead-end job with no possibilities of advancement but even there you can use the skills offered there in your next employment. The most important thing is to be yourself and keep your eyes and focus on Christ.

ARE YOU WAITING ON GOD, OR IS HE WAITING ON YOU?

> God just might be waiting on you to make the first move

Have you ever thought that God just might be waiting on you to make the first move so that He can do a work in your life? If a man gets out of his car struggling to change a tire, more than likely someone will stop to help but as long as he sits in the car with the flat tire, he will probably fall sleep and the tire will remain flat. If a man is struggling to push his broken-down car out of the road, more than likely he will get help but if he just sits in the car with a flat tire, he will probably only get loud horns blowing at him.

Think about it,

* The Red Sea did not part until Moses held up his staff.
* The walls of Jericho did not come down until they marched around the walls several times.
* Peter did not walk on water until he stepped out of the boat.

They all had to do something first before an action was made. While you are waiting on God, He is waiting on you to step out on faith or for you to make an initial effort. You have got to believe that God wants to make a shifting in your life and the last thing that should be holding you back is you being afraid to step out. Start thinking positive.

When my wife and I moved into our first apartment, we were thrilled but even then we were already thinking about building a house. When our first child was born we were already thinking about college life for her. You have to think positive and not let your current situation become your norm. Take the first step and God will lead and guide you in taking the rest.

When my wife and I recently left Texas moving to Tennessee, you talk about stepping out on faith? Our house in Texas by contract and being sold so quickly put us in a situation where we had to prematurely move out.

The new house in Tennessee was not completely finished and to make things more difficult, the loan for the new house had not even been finalized and approved. But there we were traveling down the highway headed to Tennessee, hoping and praying that the home would be completed in a timely manner and that we would get approved for the loan. We had no other choice but to go by faith, put our trust in God and keep moving forward.

> "Trust in the Lord with all thine heart; and
> lean not unto thine own understanding. In
> all thy ways acknowledge Him, and He shall
> direct thy path" (Proverbs 3:5-6 KJV).

We were both devastated but still praising God and it was not until after we had driven half the distance from Texas to Tennessee that the loan officer called to inform us that the loan for the new house was approved and we could close the following day and a hour later the builder called and stated that we could move into the brand-new home in two days! I pulled that car over to the curb and we began to praise and worship God like never before!

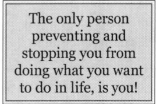

The only person preventing and stopping you from doing what you want to do in life, is you!

Actually, before we had received all the good news we were planning to stay with family members living in another state if things did not go as planned. I tell you we serve a very awesome GOD, he has always come through and has always been on time!

There are going to be times throughout your life when you are going to have to step out on faith and just go for it. What do you have to lose? At least give it a try. Apply for the house you desire, take the vacation you have been dreaming of. Heck, go ahead and marry that person you have been dating for the past seven or so years. The only person preventing and stopping you from doing what you want to do, is you. God is waiting on you to take one step and He will take the rest.

If we didn't step out on faith at that period of time, we would have greatly regretted it because soon after we left Texas many of those open doors for us began to close, interest rate rose, not to mention the huge snow storm you remember that completely shut down Texas in 2020. Sometimes God will open a window of opportunity for you to make a move and that window will also eventually close.

Many times we miss out by not recognizing the window of opportunity. I will say it again, God is waiting on you to take one step forward and He will be by your side to help you alone the way to complete your journey, just try Him.

IT'S YOUR MOVE!

There was a time when our entire church was praising and worshipping. I looked around and noticed that even though the spirit was moving in a mighty way but no one was really getting filled. No hands raised, no praise dancing nothing. God spoke to me and said, "Stop looking around and keep your eyes and focus on me!" I closed my eyes raised my hands and I began to worship not worrying about who saw me or what they were thinking. A minute later everyone was doing the same.

Maybe you are waiting on God to move in your life before you will step out thinking that perhaps you may fail. Maybe you are a faithful person and you know that God will provide because He is always right on time. Maybe you think that the perfect opportunity will come after a few more years of experience. Waiting on God ha?, Maybe, just maybe God is waiting on you to make the first move.

Reflection and Relevant Questions

1. Has there ever been a time in your life when you actually heard God speaking to you to step out on faith and you failed to take advantage of the situation and later regretted it? Explain.
2. Do you have a quiet place in your home? A place of peace, relaxation a place where you can separate yourself from the cares of the world. A place where you can talk privately with God. Tell about that special place.
3. Personally, what do you expect out of life? Do you feel that you have achieved all or some of the goals you set out to accomplish years ago? List some of those goals you planned for and have achieved/those you are still working on.

6

>> >> >> >> >> >> « « « « « « «

I WILL FOLLOW YOU!

Then said Jesus unto His disciples, If any man will
come after me, let him deny himself, and take up
his cross and follow me (Matthew 16:24 KJV).

s I mentioned earlier, several years ago my wife and I moved from, Ohio to Texas which was over a thousand-mile drive by car. Her car was loaded down and so was mine. We had driven more than half the distance when out of nowhere we drove straight into this huge tornado like storm.

Suddenly we noticed cars pulling off to the side of the road and we were in the midst of several car accidents. As the storm was getting stronger and destroying everything in its path, the waters on the highway continued to rise to what seemed to be over a half a foot deep. From experience, I kept my tires in the water pathways the truck in front of me were making.

My wife and I kept communicating through our newly brought cell phones and the signal was going in and out. Even though she was driving directly behind me, we could barely see each other because the rain was coming down so hard. She said, "Paul the rain is blinding me, I can't see your car pull over!"

Knowing that the tornado had turned and was now coming up from behind us, we had no choice but to keep pushing and driving forward. I responded back to my wife, "Keep your tires in the water tracks that my car is making from the rain and follow me babe, we can get through this."

By God's grace we made it through the storm and later found out that what we went through was a major tornado stretching over two miles wide causing several people to die from it. Following and driving in the tracks of the car in front of me during big rain storms was one of the driving techniques my father taught me when I was in his driving school for beginners.

CONSIDER THE COST

There is a benefit when it comes to following or being a follower which at times can be a necessity for example when you and

> In order to be an effective leader, you must first be an effective follower!

other vehicles are traveling together and at other times following will be required, especially when it comes to following Our Lord and Savior, Jesus Christ. Besides that, in order to be an effective leader, you must first be an effective follower. Most professional coaches were once the assistant coach where they learned and followed a lot of the patterns coming from the Head coach. Most Senior Pastors were once Assistant Pastor learning from the Senior Pastor at one time or another, all had to be a follower before taking on the leadership role.

We find so too many instances throughout the New Testament where Jesus has said, *Come follow me*."

* He says to Peter and Andrew, "Follow me" (Matthew 4:19 kjv).
* Jesus says to a rich young ruler, "Come and follow me" (Matthew 19:21 kjv).
* He says to Matthew the tax collector, "Follow me" (Matthew 9:9 kjv).

When Jesus says, "Come follow me" it is not a command but rather an invitation. An invitation requiring submitting your entire self to Him and learning and applying His teachings through the help of the Holy Spirit into your own life. Submission is not an act of weakness, it simply means relinquishing your authority and being under the authority of someone else which is a strong characteristic.

Jesus is our everything: Our provider, Our comforter, Our protector, Our teacher, Our everything! Who else could offer so much and ask for so little? We are required to follow His instructions, live by His ways and simply put, to be more like Him. We are living in perilous times and in the last days. What else needs to be said, Take up your cross, submit yourself to Jesus and follow Him!

But hold on, before you can consider following and being a vessel for Christ, you must first consider the cost! Salvation is free but, the Anointing is going to cost you something. You are going to have to go through things before God's anointing can fall upon you.

Many years ago my wife and I considered building our first new home. We sat down and tried to plan it all out. We had narrowed it down to seven homes. But after figuring in the rising cost of materials, labor and land, that plan was narrowed down to two.

Building a new home is very expensive. For if we would have started building our new home without first considering the cost and half way running out of money, it would have been considered a failure.

> Before you can consider following and being a vessel for Christ you must first consider the cost!

On the other hand, before you consider being a vessel and a follower of Christ, you must first consider the cost, the cost is very high! The Bible says in the book of Luke:

> "If any man come to me, and hate not his father, and mother, and his wife, and children, and brethren, and sisters, yea, and his own life also, he cannot be my disciple. And whosoever doth not bear his cross, and come after me, cannot be my disciple. For which of

you, intending to build a tower, sitteth not down first
and counteth the cost, whether he have sufficient to
finish it?" (Luke 14:26-28 KJV)

That is a pretty big price to pay, would you agree?

God said to Abraham, "Get thee out of thy country, and from thy
kindred, and from thy father's house, unto a land that I will shew
thee." (Genesis 12:1 KJV). Abraham obeyed and did what he was told

> You must be
> willing to give
> up everything
> for Jesus!

Jesus, walking by the sea of Galilee
saw two brethren, Simon called Peter, and
Andrew his brother, casting a net into the
sea: for they were fishers. And He saith
unto them, "Follow me, and I will make
you fishers of men"(Matt: 4:19 KJV). They dropped their nets, obeyed
and followed Jesus.

Yes, the cost is very high considering the fact that you must give
up family and all worldly inheritance. You must be willing to give up
everything for Jesus. It requires a emptying of yourself so that Jesus
can fill you with the glory of Himself. You must strive every day to
be more like Him.

But also remember that there is no cost you pay in becoming
a vessel for Christ that won't be made up of a thousandfold in the
resurrection, this is also a fact!

It is imperative for you to know that Jesus will never force you to
do anything. Making the decision to do his Will and to follow Him
is totally up to you but, there are consequences and a cost that comes
when you decide to disobey and not listen to Him.

You remember what happened to Jonah? God told him to go and
prophesy to the inhabitants of Nineveh but, instead, he attempted
to flee from the presence of the Lord by going to Joppa and he was
swallowed up by a giant fish (Jonah 1:17 kjv).

You remember what happened to Lot's wife? The angels of the
Lord warned Lot and his family to leave Sodom and to not look
back? While they were leaving the city, Lot's wife decided to look

back at the burning city and she was turned into a pillar of salt (Gen. 19:26 kjv).

Why is it so hard for us to listen, follow and obey instructions especially when a Word is spoken directly to you from God? Is not God speaking loud enough? Do you always need a confirmation from God or are you hearing clearly and loudly and you choose to rather simply ignore? I'm telling you, that is very dangerous. At what cost are you willing to sacrifice in order to start walking in His was? To what extent are you willing to go to follow Jesus?

> To what extent are you willing to go to follow Jesus?

PUT TO THE TEST

When I was younger may be nine or ten, our family went to visit one of my Mothers uncles in Georgia whom she had not seen in over thirty years. My brother and I were so delighted because this was our first time visiting the state. The smell, the atmosphere and even the way peoples spoke was totally different from that of Ohio what I was familiar with.

After meeting some of our cousins our age I did not know whether to laugh or feel sorry because of the way they spoke. My Dad who was raised in the south had to remind us that we all have different accents and we sometimes refer to things differently. The people in the south speak differently than those in the north but it all means the same. He gave us a few examples. In Ohio you call a can of soda, "soda", in Georgia they call it, "pop." In Ohio you say, "Let's go for a ride" in Georgia you may say, "Let's hit a block" things are said differently but still mean the same. After Dad explained, I understood.

I felt that it was going to take some time getting adjusted to that. After visiting my Moms relatives and walking and sight-seeing all day, we were all tired and wore out. As night finally came we all headed to our rooms for the night. As my brother and I laid in the comfortable bed going over the day's events we noticed that someone had dropped money on the floor. We picked it all up which was about seven dollars in change.

> Have you ever been tested or tried by God?

We looked at each other wondering what we should do with our newly found wealth. We could buy lots of stuff, snacks, toys whatever then, we thought about the leather belt holding up our Dads pants and we instantly dropped the change back on the floor and went to sleep.

The next morning Uncle Walt came into our room and sat next to us on the bed. He reached down and grabbed the change that was on the floor and counted it and looked at us and smiled. Reaching in his back pocket he took out his wallet. He gave my brother and myself ten dollars each along with all the change on the floor. Uncle Walt said that he had intentionally placed the change on the floor the night before just to see if we would take it or not, to test our honesty.

Have you ever been tested before? Had feelings that you were being tested by God Himself? The time you found a wallet lying on the ground. The time you were given back too much change after buying something. Have you ever felt that your obedience, honesty and faith were being tested?

Abraham was a man being tested. Abraham before being converted by God was called Abram. God said to Abram, "Get thee out of thy country, and from thy father's house, unto a land that I will shew thee"(Genesis 12:1 kjv). As you can see here how God is testing Abram's *obedience* to see if he would leave his family and go to an unknown place, a place that he was unfamiliar with and has never been.

Next, during his journey to this unknown land with his nephew Lot, there became an issue in regards to the massive size of Abrams livestock and Lots livestock's availability of water. Abram recognized that he and Lot had to separate-Abram went one way and Lot went the other. Here you can see how Abrams *faith* was being tested to see if he had enough faith to go on this journey alone.

And finally, Abraham's final test came in regards to his beloved son Isaac and I will show you exactly how it is written in the scripture:

"God said unto Abraham, take now thy son, thine only son Isaac whom thou lovest, and get thee into the land of Moriah; and offer him there for a burnt offering upon one of the mountains which I will tell thee of."(Genesis 22:2 kjv)

Abraham had a problem. God told Abraham to take his son Isaac up to the mountain so he could be sacrificed. Isaac was probably use to his father making and giving sacrifices to God so this was no big issue. Isaac gathered the wood, helped carry it to the sight and even helped build an alter and light the fire.

Isaac looked around asked "Where is the sacrificial lamb for the burnt offering" and Abraham looked back at him and said, "God will provide for himself a lamb for a burnt offering." Can you feel the fear in poor Isaac? Abraham went ahead and tied Isaac up and laid him on the alter preparing to do what God had instructed.

He stretched his hand and took the knife and at that very moment an angel of the Lord said, *"Lay not thine hand upon the lad, neither do thou anything unto him: for now I know that thou fearest God"*(Genesis 22:12 kjv). Abraham looked up and saw a ram caught in the thicket by its horns which he used for the burnt offering instead of his son.

> The Holy Spirit will guide you in a positive direction that will be pleasing to God.

As you can see here how Abrahams *obedience and faithfulness* is being tested again. The answer to Abrahams problem was already supplied. On one side of the mountain was the problem and on the other side was the answer. God always has a solution to problem even before the problem arises in our lives.

As you can see even with Abrahams dilemma, it involved a mountain. God will give us a mountain to get you to the next level or a place of rest. Think of Noah, the Bible says: "And the ark rested in the seventh month, on the seventeenth day of the month, upon the mountains of Ararat"(Gen. 8:4kjv). God is saying, "Go to the mountains."

Sometimes God will not only test our faithfulness and honesty but will also test us on how we handle ourselves in certain situations. He knows that we are going to make mistakes, a lot of them. But, He has given us the Holy Spirit that will convict us and guide us in a positive direction that will be pleasing to Him. At the same time, because we have so many options, we on occasion may get tested just to make sure that we are still being faithful and obedient and are on the same page with Him.

Reflection and Relevant Questions

1. Have you ever found yourself in a position where being a follower was more beneficial to you and others as opposed to you being the leader? Explain
2. Name a time when you felt that you were being tested by others/ by God.
3. At what Cost or Sacrifice are you willing to make in order to be a Vessel for Christ and to follow Him?

7

>>»»»» «««««««

FLEEING FROM YOUTHFUL LUST

Flee also from youthful lust; but pursue
righteousness, faith, love, peace with those
who call on the Lord out of a pure heart
(2 Timothy 2:22 KJV).

LOVE AND LUST

lthough God wants us to have nice things and the
wants of our hearts desires, we must remember to
keep our eyes on Jesus. Whatever we keep our eyes
on-we will direct majority of
our focus on. Keeping our eyes on Jesus keeps
us and protects us from lustful desires. On
the other hand, if we keep our eyes focused
on the wrong things, it will keep us under

> Love is giving
> and purity and
> lust is sin.

its control. You have to agree that there is a big difference between
love and lust. The Bible says, (Flee also youthful lust: but pursue
righteous, faith, love, peace, with those who call on the Lord out of a
pure heart (2 Timothy 2:22). Love is giving and purity and lust is sin.
Love develops and lust destroys. Love is peaceful and lust is dead to

passion and creates anxiety. You don't have to fulfil the sin of lust, focus your mind on Christ.

You remember the trials that Joseph went through? He was brought as a slave by Potiphar one of Pharaohs guards. He was seduced by Potiphars wife, but Joseph eluded her and she falsely accused him of assaulting her, and he was sent to prison. While in prison it became known that he could interpret dreams. He interpreted Pharaohs dream and Pharaoh promoted Joseph to be second in command over Egypt under him. He did not allow the spirit of lust to take control over his mind. You have to recognize and see lust for what it is and flee from it just as Joseph did.

In every airport there is a control tower. The Air traffic controller reviews the weather and flight plan to insure safe, orderly flow of air traffic. Your mind is a control tower, it controls what you see, how you perceive it and how you will react to certain situations. In the control tower you decide destinations and you decide what you want to be and what you want to accomplish in life.

There is a cost for giving into the spirit of lust. It always lead to a downward spiral. You have to make the decision to follow Christ or not, I pray that you make the decision to follow Christ!

What motivates you? In other words, what in life whether it be a person, place or thing that pushes and drives you to do just a little bit more rather than if it were simply left up to you, you would have done the least amount of work or effort possible? In my younger years it was my parents who motivated me whom I loved to please and see the smile on their faces when I had done something good.

Maybe it was cleaning up my room or washing dishes without being told. As I got a little older and motivators became a bit harder. I was rewarded with a new bike or a new outfit without it being my birthday or Christmas. Rewarded for bringing home and decent report card or following instructions they gave.

As a teenager and having my first job, it was a new day when I received my first paycheck. I felt as though I was a full fledge adult especially after my Dad helped me to open up a bank account. I learned to be on time never late and do what I was told and if I did that, I could receive a good check. Slowly money was becoming my motivation. I would work day and night looking forward to the next payday. Working was my incentive, money was my motivation and buying things was making me happy and I was completely satisfied

I remember during an interview, one of the richest men in the entire world was asked the question: "How much money would it take for you to say that you have enough money?" His answer: "Just one more dollar." Meaning that he would never have enough money to satisfy his wants and needs.

BOASTING

It always feel good to talk about the good times or the good things that are happening in our lives. A recent achievement, a recent promotion or even the birthing of a new child, we all love to talk and brag about our grandchildren even about a high school game you played in thirty years ago, the good things in our lives, who doesn't?

> Boast on how God has opened doors for you when all before they seemed permanently closed!

But, are these the things that God wants us to be bragging about or boasting on? It is one thing when other folks talk good about you or even brag about what a good job you did but, it is another thing when you yourself have to constantly bring up the good things you have achieved.

Sometimes when you think that you are speaking highly or boasting on certain things, have you ever thought that you could possibly be offending someone or worse, not be pleasing to God. It can easily happen.

You don't boast about your wealth and power or your position at your job but instead boast on how God has opened doors for you when all before they seemed permanently closed. You don't boast about how long you have been a faithful member of the church, but instead talk about how your relationship with Christ has continued to increase abundantly over the years.

Boasting on anything especially on yourself gives credit to you and takes away the glory from God.

It is sad to think that society has conditioned us to believe that the more you have the less you need God and the less that you have the more you need God, why is that?

Listen here, why is there a need to brag or boast upon anything anyway? Boasting is showing pride, glorifying yourself and most times trying to improve your reputation. But, remember this, your reputation is only as good as the popularity of you. Once your popularity is gone, your reputation is all but forgotten about as well.

> "For men shall be lovers of themselves, lovers of money, boastful, proud, blasphemers, disobedient to parents, unthankful, unholy"
> Tim 3:2 kjv

The bottom line my dear reader is that, God is desiring you to brag about how you have made His priorities your priorities, that's all!

Reflection and Relevant Questions

1. What is the biggest temptation you had to face in life (whether it be lust, money, material things)and how did you overcome it?
2. Why do you feel that certain people tend to have a strong need to constantly brag on themselves? Explain
3. What motivates you or what are the most influential things in your life?

PART II

THE HEART OF A VESSEL

A Vessel of Honor is one who openly exemplifies
and carries out the purposeful will of God
under the leadership of His son Jesus Christ.

8

>»»»»»» ««««««««

A GRATEFUL HEART

"Be careful for nothing; but in everything by
prayer and supplication with thanksgiving, let your
request be known unto God. And the peace of
God, which passeth all understanding, shall keep
your hearts and minds through Christ Jesus."
(Philippians 4:6-7 KJV)

hrough all of my trials and tribulations I have learned
to be grateful and thankful for everything that occurs
in my life because things could have been a whole lot
more worse than what I experienced. Have you ever
thought that things were so bad that you were going to jump out of
your skin? Believe me there are hundreds of people who you may
even know personally who are ready, willing and able to gladly jump
into your skin and take your place, right now. Gratitude is everything.
Even during the worst of times, you can find something to be thankful
for. We have to learn to be grateful and thankful and continue to give
God thanks and praise because He alone is deserving!.

But what does it really mean to be grateful? What does it really
mean to have a heart of gratitude? So many people today believe in
chance rather than God. They believe that, "Well, I took this medicine
and now I am healed, my healing could possibly have come from

the medicines or it could have come from God." This is not having a grateful heart towards the medicines or God, the healing could possibly have come about simply, by *chance*. So who or what do you show gratitude towards, you being healed or the healer? The pills or God?

Let me tell you about one gentleman who showed appreciation, gratefulness and a heart of gratitude all together.

Jesus was known for His teachings, offering human salvation and eternal life but unlike anything else-Healing. This included spiritual healing as well as physical healing. But, how often do we read about someone saying "Thank You for healing me" or showing any appreciation for what Jesus did for them?

On His way to Jerusalem, Jesus had to pass through the cities of Samaria and Galilee and He encountered ten men who had a problem, they had a skin condition called leprosy. During those days anyone who had leprosy was considered to be an outcast and until present days it was a chronic and incurable disease therefore they had to go to the priest for examination who would then decide if they were clean or unclean before being accepted back into the community.

When these ten men found out that Jesus was visiting their town they cried out and yelled from a distance, "Jesus, Master, have mercy on us!"(Luke 17:12-13 kjv) They cried out and asked for mercy because they knew that Jesus was only passing through and they did not want to miss this once in a life time opportunity and felt that they may never see Him again.

You see here in the scripture, the ten lepers did not ask to be healed, they asked for mercy. Sometimes God will give you what you need more than what you ask for. Jesus demonstrated it and told them to show themselves to the priest and as they went, they were healed and cleansed of their disease. After being healed they went their way all but one who turned and went back to Jesus.

> Sometimes God will give you more of what you need than what you ask for!

Now, why would you think that this one gentleman would turn and go back to Jesus? Did he feel that he did not get completely healed? Did he lose or forget something and was going back to retrieve it? No, he turned and went back and fell at Jesus feet praising and worshipping wanting to simply tell Jesus, "THANK YOU!"

> "Lord, I Thank You for healing me! All that I have been through Lord, Thank you. I was considered an outcast because of my disease and You lord healed me, Jesus I just came back to say, "Thank You." When I did not have money to pay bills and you made a way for them to get paid and You provided food on my table, Lord I just came back to say, "Thank You!"

The worse thing we can do with what God has given or done for us is showing lack of appreciation. Appreciation causes the value of anything to increase. There are going to be times in your life my dear reader, when you are going to have to turn and go back and tell somebody, "Thank You." You don't have to stand at a distance, you don't have to yell and scream from the top of your lungs for Jesus to hear you because He is always next to you.

All you have to do is call upon Him and He will answer you. You remember reading in the above scripture, Jesus did not touch or even tell the ten lepers that they were healed, He told them to go and show themselves to the priest. They were already healed but failed to simply say, "Thank You."

There are times in life when you will need to tell somebody, "Thank You."

In regards to our Lord Jesus Christ, we also need to show our appreciation and gratitude towards Him every hour and every minute of the day on a daily basis, and simply say:

"Jesus I Thank You,"

For my bills getting paid, "Jesus, I just want to say, Thank You."

For providing food on the table, "Jesus, I just want to say, Thank You."

For protecting my family, "Jesus, I just want to say, Thank You."

For healing my body, "Jesus, I just want to say, Thank You"

This shows appreciation, this shows gratitude for what Jesus has done and what He is going to do in your life and those surrounding you.

BE CONTENT

There are people who have worked their entire life to save as much money as possible in 401's, retirement funds so that one day they can live that American dream to retire lying on someone's beach watching the sun go down.

The reality for many though is that once they finally reach the age of retirement with a bank full of money they have settled down relaxing then all at once their feet start hurting, back pain kicking in and God forbitten living alone, now what? I have seen it time after time where folks have retired and only after a year or so they go back to working from being bored.

Money is not the solution nor is it a remedy for you to receive happiness in your life. Happiness comes from the result of something happening. Joy comes from the Lord. Happiness is external, Joy is internal. Your true happiness will only come from you searching within yourself. To tell the truth, the most sincere joyful people are the ones who have the least. If you compare people living in the poorest nations to those who have it all you will notice that those who smile the most, those who are most grateful and content are the ones having very little.

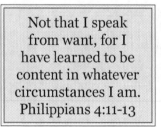

Not that I speak from want, for I have learned to be content in whatever circumstances I am. Philippians 4:11-13

I think that I mentioned it before within this book regarding a televised interview that was held with one of the richest men in the world. He was asked the question, "How much money would it take for you to say ok, I have enough?" His answer, "Just one more dollar." What he was saying is that there will never be enough money to satisfy his need of wanting just a little bit more. We have to be grateful and content with what God has allowed us to have and enjoy at this present moment.

"Not that I speak in respect of want: for I have learned,
in whatsoever state I am, therewith to be content"
(Philippians 4:11 KJV).

The Bible says *in* everything give thanks but in the book of Ephesians chapter four it takes it a little further, it says to give thanks *for* all things. You have to learn to be content and give thanks for whatever situation you may be experiencing, things can always be worse. Raise your hands and give God thanks because He is worthy of our praise, no matter what you are going through give Him praise! You know I am right!

REASONING

What is reasoning? I came up with this explanation especially as a youth growing up. "Reasoning" occurs when a person tries to figure out the "whys" and "what's" of situations in an attempt to get a clearer understanding of it. One of these situations occurred for me when I was maybe six or seven years old. My Dad and I would often have these Man to boy talks and sometimes on occasion I would get to speak.

One time I remember quite clearly is the time I tried to explain to him the reason as to why I did not like going to school, I did not think that it was important and I wanted to quit that very day, ok I was nine.

He listened patiently as I explained in detail that getting up early, riding a school bus, and sitting hour after hour in a classroom to a teacher was unnecessary, "Why can't I just get a job, make money like you" I said. He just sat on the couch with a smile on his face until I was finished talking and I had gotten everything out that was on my mind.

When I was finally finished, he said, "Let me tell you a little story boy. When I was your age, I did not have the opportunity to attend school. My eight brothers and I had no choice but to go out and work with our father in the cotton fields. I was only seven years old the same age as you are right now. I not only had to pick cotton but I also

85

had to clean pig pins and eat foods that you would probably consider throwing away today.

The few days out of the year that I was allowed to attend school which were far and in between, I had to walk because there were no school buses at least for us there were none, and it did not matter if it was a foot of snow or the ground was one hundred degrees hot under my bear feet, I had to walk to school. Life was very hard during those days and you young people these days do not have a clue or appreciate how well off you have it today."

When my Dad finished talking to me, I thought about all the luxuries and comfort not only myself were enjoying but everyone I knew were enjoying and we were taking it all for granted. We as vessels for Christ have to be reasonable and mindful and not take things for granted.

In all actuality, when I looked back and thought about it for a moment, I could not remember a day we did not have lights in the house except for when the entire neighborhood was out. Could not remember a day going without food or clean clothes to wear.

Actually, me going to school in the 70's and 80's we complained when the school bus was three minute's late or the route was pushed one street further than usual to accommodate another student. We were not only being unreasonable but being inconsiderate of others taking for granted even having a school bus to ride.

Reasoning requires you to think of things in a logical way. Every day of our lives is going to require some form of reasoning. It is going to require you to take a step back, look around and recognize the blessings and be grateful for what God has done for you.

DROP THE PRIDE

"Pride goeth before destruction, and a haughty spirit before a fall" (Prov. 16:18kjv).

Several years ago, my wife and I traveled to Nevada to celebrate one of our wedding anniversaries. We had been travelling on the airplane for what seemed like days but in reality, it was only four hours and we were excited once we landed. As we walked through the terminal, I noticed a couple sitting on a bench. As we got closer, I realized that it was actually the father and mother sitting on the bench and their two children were lying under the bench sound asleep covered under a blanket.

As people walked past the bench some would offer money and help to the family. To my surprise the father would raise his hand saying, "No thank you." I thought to myself, "If the family is homeless, children cold and hungry why not at least take a few dollars offered and buy some food?" The Bible speaks on that very issue, "Pride goeth before destruction, and a haughty spirit before a fall." (Proverbs. 16:18 kjv)

But, the father not even looking up refused everything offered to the family including shelter, food and money. Is that something you would consider or call pride or something else?

My father once corrected me on something similar that I have never forgotten. While on one of our fishing excursions we had all gotten extremely soaked from the rain. One of his friends offered me one of his dry shirts and I said, "No I don't want it." My Dad did not show any expressions until we had gotten home later that he expressed his disappointment in me.

His frustrations with me was in regards to me turning down the shirt that his friend had offered to me earlier. My Daddy said, "Look here son, when someone offers you something, you take it, and if you really do not want or like the offer someone is giving you, you can get rid of it later, not in front of them."

It took a while for me to fully comprehend that statement but after thinking it over I understood it completely. When someone offers you anything, you accept it gratefully because you just don't know it possibly could have been their very best or their very last and for you to turn it down could be heartbreaking for them.

Besides that, by you refusing an offer, you could possibly be blocking a blessing that the good Lord was about to bestow upon them but you are blocking it. Be an open Vessel, when someone is offering you something, it is an act of kindness and shows love, something we all need to be practicing more of.

BE WILLING TO HELP OTHERS

Recently a relative of mine had made a visit to our home and we talked for a while. I asked him how work was going and he replied that it was going well. He had become a supervisor and we began talking about how work ethics have changed over the years especially during the covid-19 epidemic.

I had mentioned to him that because of the covid epidemic many of the experienced workers either quit or retired forcing restaurants and other establishments to hire unskilled teenagers paying them higher wages than experienced adults resulting in the quality of food and service less than satisfactory.

My relative had a different aspect regarding work ethics. He mentioned that several specific coworkers working under his supervision who not only had excellent work ethics but also a comradery and bond they had just among themselves. These five gentlemen who happen to be from a country in Africa were very hard workers and actually stood together and helped each other through everything while at home and at work.

What stood out was that these five guys who had not yet established health insurance or bank accounts had actually made a pot in which they each would put money into it each week so that whenever one of them needed help the money was available. It could have been for late rent, bills, or whatever they needed it for it did not matter, but that same person had to eventually replace it and continue to put money back into the pot each week so that money was there if any one of them ever needed financial help it was available. I thought about that how people help each other.

WHAT ABOUT US?

When my wife and I lived in Texas, we had great neighbors. Our neighbors across the street from us had recently moved from Mexico. When they first moved into their three-bedroom home there were twelve people living there. Over time the numbers began to dwindle down and the only ones left was the two parents and their two children.

After some time and getting acquainted with each other I asked the father what happened to the rest of the family? He replied, "Oh, they were not all family, but some were. The way we were taught from a child is to help each other. If one person brought a home, family, friends could stay there until they were able to better themselves and were able to help someone else and the cycle would go on" now I thought to myself, "That's deep."

I see so much of this in people from other countries but what about the people in this country who were born, raised and live here? Where is the help, where is the comradery? You want a house, you have to go out there and work hard, save money and get it for yourself.

Not to mention getting help to build it. I just hope that you have saved enough money to pay someone to build it. What about going to a neighbor asking for food? I hope that you have planted a garden to grow your own or you have money to buy food. There seems to be little help for people these days and it seems like every man is out for himself. But, that is not the way God wants it.

Many years ago, I asked my father for something he had and he said to me, "GOD bless the child who has his own." That statement was not meant to be harsh or mean towards me at all, but what my father was saying is that "It is better for you to work hard and obtain things on your own, you will appreciate it more." Not bad advice at all ha?

Reflection and Relevant Questions

1. Has your ego or pride cause you to not do something or do something because of people around were watching but in your heart, you knew differently? Explain.
2. In what ways are you helping others not expecting anything in return.
3. When was the last time you truly said "Thank You" to Jesus not for what He has done but for who He is?

9

>>>>>>>> «««««««

PRACTICE FORGIVENESS

"Then came Peter to Him, and said, Lord, how oft
shall my brother sin against me, and I forgive him?
Till seven times? Jesus saith unto him, "I say not unto
thee, Until seven times: but, Until seven times seven
(Matthew 18:21-22 KJV)

erhaps one of the most difficult feelings to overcome
for many of us is that of unforgiveness. You get sad
and soon get over it. You have thoughts of loneliness
and soon get over it. But, believe it or not, a person
can hurt your feelings in a conversation or with one simple word and
you can hold a grudge or unforgiveness in your heart towards them
for days, years and for some even a lifetime!

I have actually known people who have gotten offended by
someone and they still hold that same bitterness in their heart towards
them over twenty years later, what is that? That says a lot about you.
You have unforgiveness towards a church member because they said
something you didn't like, you can't forgive another parent because
their child had a conflict with yours. While the children have made
up years ago and are getting along, both parents are still not speaking.

That one particular incident that was so hurtful has been on your
heart for so long that you don't even remember the details of what

actually happened, you only remember, the hurt. Your heart has gotten so stiff and harden that it's hard for you to forgive someone even when you try to.

This may be one of the hardest things you ever do in life but you have to break that spirit of unforgiveness and holding grudges against people and allow God to come into your heart and do a work in you so that you can start forgiving others and you can find some relief in your heart!

You will recognize true forgiveness in your heart when you can sit in between two grudgeful people who are against you and have total peace within yourself. If there is no peace, then unforgiveness is still has a place in your heart.

> If there is no peace, then unforgiveness still has a place in your heart!

I always wondered why it is so hard to be kind or to forgive? Is it because not forgiving someone or ignoring them is easier than simply saying "I forgive you?" Or perhaps you never really cared for the person in the first place so not forgiving them is just another way of escape? Whatever the case may be, unforgiveness is real and it is not what The Lord wants for you and I.

The Bible says:

> "And be ye kind one to another, tenderhearted,
> forgiving one another, even as God for Christ sake
> hath forgiven you" (Ephesians 4:32 KJV).

Have you ever thought that same person who was sitting on the corner holding a homeless sign asking for a dollar you decided to ignore could possibly later on be the same person to give you a dollar while you are standing in front of a crowded cashiers line being short of a dollar?

Worse than that, suppose that very same person who you have decided not to forgive end up being your neighbor in heaven, how would you look at them then?

We have to practice kindness and forgiveness towards our fellow man or woman. Forgiveness shows quality and your true character.

Forgiveness softens your heart and opens you up to receive blessings from God.

FORGIVING YOURSELF

Why does it always seem like the hardest person to forgive is not the person who lied on you, not the person who abused you, not even the person who mistreated you? That one person who you fail to forgive for everything that has ever happened to you, is YOU!

Forgiveness always seems to come easy especially when it comes to someone else but when it comes to forgiving ourself, we find it hard.

The fact of the matter is that you can say that you forgave someone and you can pretend to have moved on, but in reality, you truly haven't forgiven them because you can't fully forgive someone else until you have first forgiven the most important person of all, You.

Self-forgiveness requires empathy and understanding as you try to work out certain areas in your life or the part you possibly played in the incident or situation.

Forgiving yourself means more than just simply putting a certain event or something from the past behind you and moving on, it is a feeling that only you can fix and requires you to accept what happened and having compassion upon yourself which is probably one of the initial steps of forgiving anyone especially yourself!

We have all been there, perhaps you accidently shared a friends personal secret and it became known around the town and you now feel guilty? Maybe you were in a crowd and you innocently and jokingly said something about someone and everyone is laughing but you and the intended person and now you feel like a jerk.

That same incident keeps playing over and over in your head and you can't get over it. You have tried to apologize, you have asked for forgiveness wanting to make up but the hurt and damage has already been done. Now the feeling of guilty has set in and you feel the need to forgive yourself for what happened.

> Forgiveness and Reconciliation requires repentance.

Forgiveness and Reconciliation requires repentance, you asking God to forgive you for allowing yourself to ever feel that way towards them in the first place. After you have done all you can, as hard as it might be, you just might have to stop trying and let go and let GOD intervene.

Believe me when I say that HE can work things out a whole lot better than you and I ever could. When you allow God to step in and you are so desiring for someone to accept your forgiveness, God knows what is best and will work on self-forgiveness first because you can't forgive anyone else until you first forgive yourself, right?

Actually, it may take you to act first or apologize in order for walls to be broken down even when you feel that you have done nothing wrong! What will it hurt for you to humble yourself and be the bigger person to apologize?

STRENGTH IN HUMBLENES

Her name was Sis Kim. We never knew her last name, all the congregation knew as Sister Kim. She was our Minister for several years before she had gotten transferred. My wife Elaina and I were searching for a church home in Cincinnati and she came into our life seemingly unexpected.

At that time my wife was working at a healthcare facility as an Activity Director and planned activities for the patients. One week a church arrived and asked if they could come speak, pray, and talk about the Bible with the patients from time to time, which was nothing unusual. Immediately, they were placed on the calendar planner.

This was during I believe to be our seventh year of being married and we were going through many trials as many new couples experience those first few trying years. Anyway, on my wife's lunch break, she went into the Activity Directors closet to pray.

Unknowingly to my wife, Sister Kim entered the closet as well and asked if she could pray for Elaina and they prayed together. We still wonder to this day how Sister Kim knew that Elaina was in the closet or that she even needed prayer? God knows everything, we will leave it at that.

They became acquainted with each other and after sometime we as a family were invited to their church which happened to be Pentecostal and we soon joined. Besides being a great teacher of the Gospel, Sister Kim was also perhaps one of the most kindest, most humblest persons we had ever met. She listened and gave advice to you like no one else as if coming straight from heaven.

No matter how busy Sister Kim was at that particular moment, she always had time to stop and pray. Her voice was always welcoming, pleasantly soft with a smile, and when she spoke everyone stopped what they were doing to listen to her. We felt as though she made only us believers in the Cincinnati area to feel special but we were totally wrong.

During the end of the yearly convention meetings, ministers would allow believers to come to the alter for prayers from the church ministers. Many of the male ministers had ten to fifteen people in line waiting to receive prayers or a word from the Lord.

When I looked at Sister Kim's prayer line, fifty to sixty believers were waiting in line to receive prayers from her! What makes people stand out like that? Was it her personality? Was it her humbleness and patience she had with people? Maybe, it was simply the God in her that everyone had seen!

> To be humble is not to think less of oneself, but to think of oneself a little less

That has been over twenty years ago until she had gotten transferred. You don't meet or find people like that every day! Actually, we thought that she was only known around the Cincinnati Ohio area but we all came to know and realize that her name was known all around the whole world!

To be humble is not to think less of oneself, but to think of oneself a little less. All throughout the gospels we read about Jesus who was perhaps the most humblest person of all. Jesus carried all the qualities of humility and showed many examples we can follow. For example, He chose to come to earth as a human. He chose to obey the Father to the point of dying an embarrassing and painful death on the cross for our sins. That shows humbleness and humility.

So how can we develop humility and humbleness and become more like Jesus in our lives today? Let's dive into this subject for a moment. First, when I examined the subject of humility and being humble, I noticed several specific characteristics that all humble people had in common:

1. Humble people are good listeners (Proverbs. 12:15).

    Truly, from my experience when it comes to trying to find someone to listen to me without any interruptions, at times it had been almost impossible.

    I guess that is the reason why so many people choose to listen to the advice from someone who is considered to be more wiser and turns to a psychologist who are paid to be silent while you speak and even then, they are carefully watching the clock to remind you when your time is up.

    It takes a lot of humbleness for one even a close friend to listen to you for just five minutes without interrupting. One who is there for you and will patiently listen to you in confidence is a true friend. You can consider that person priceless.

2. They assume responsibility for their actions (Romans 3:9)

    Humble people are quick to admit and confess they were wrong in a situation when they are actually wrong. A humble person is not afraid to say, "I'm sorry" or "I made a mistake, please forgive me." That is a humble person one you can rely on.

3. They put others first (Philippians 2:3-4).

    Instead of competing or rivalry, they will rather choose to allow another person go ahead of them. They will consider others more important than themselves. They open doors for others, they make sure others are ok before they look at themself.

4. They repent of their sins (James4:8).

   A humble person will immediately repent of anything they feel may have offended their brother and especially the Lord. They are mindful of offense and carful with words and actions coming out and from them.

5. They are grateful for what they have (Thessalonians 5:8).

   You can easily recognize a humble person because they are truly thankful and grateful for what has been given them. They are content with having very little.

> Jesus is Jesus and there is no one like Him and He stands alone in His glory!

Believe me, there are some very good people in the world today who have a lot of good qualities but, Jesus Christ is the only one who has all the qualities of being totally and completely humble. Jesus is Jesus and there is no one like Him and He stands alone in His glory!

Don't get me to preaching up in here!

We are all in need of work and help in our lives and are striving to be more Christ like. Prayer is the key to humbling ourselves especially during times when we feel the need to interrupt someone or the urge to speak our minds but instead we are biting our lips trying to hold our peace. I tell you, it takes prayers, much prayers!

Reflection and Relevant Questions

1. What is the main reason as to why you find it so hard to forgive a certain person for what they did to you? Explain
2. Do you believe that certain spirits like unforgiveness and hatred can be a generational curse past down from ancestors?
3. In this chapter Paul talked about humbleness. What do you think distinguishes a humble person from one who is not humble?

10

>> >> >> >> >> >> ‹‹ ‹‹ ‹‹ ‹‹ ‹‹ ‹‹ ‹‹

STANDING ALONE

"Fear thou not; for I am with thee: be not
dismayed; for I am thy God: I will strengthen
thee; yea, I will help thee; yea, I will uphold thee
with the right hand of my righteousness."
(Isaiah 41:10 KJV)

hen I was younger, I was elected to be a member of
our City Council. We were comprised of three men
and four women. Our job was very important because
the survival of the community was dependent upon
the decisions, we seven council members made.

It was very important that we were all on one accord especially
when it came down to money matters but there was a time when one
council member stood alone and up roared the citizens, but actually
saved our community.

Every five years or so, this huge corporation, I will call (ABC
corporation) would give our community a huge grant ($50,000) which
we could use for street repairs, playgrounds for the children, activities
for seniors, housing and so on. Time had come for us to receive and
renew the usual application which we as council members would
simply sign and return. Actually, we had only three days to read over

the application, vote on it and get it back to ABC corporation which was not a problem since ABC was only a mile away.

The mayor called a special meeting so that we all could look over and sign the application, nothing unusual. Once we had signed the application it was ready to be voted on at another special council meeting the following day. The night of the special council meeting a representative from ABC company had come so that he could personally hand deliver the application back to company headquarters.

The council chambers were full to capacity with standing room only. Citizens from the neighborhood, committee members from various departments and even a news reporter were on site anxiously awaiting for the application to be voted on, signed and delivered. As each council members

> Be careful for nothing; but in everything by prayer and supplication with thanksgiving let your request be made known unto God.
> Philippians 4:6 kjv

name was called out an applause was given and everyone said "Yes" all but one council member.

Everyone in attendance held their breath in total disbelief and surprise wondering why she had voted NO on something that we as a committee and community as a whole had desperately been waiting on and in need of the for years. People started yelling and calling her out of her name. Citizens were outraged because one person had held up the vote from getting passed. The mayor publicly asked her, "Why did you do that?"

Actually, the lady held her head down on the table and started crying as if being stoned and tormented. Even I was looking at her thinking that she had made a major mistake by voting "No" on the grant that we had all previously talked about and agreed upon, what was wrong with her?

To tell you the truth, I felt kind of sorry for her myself. Her face was full of tears as she got up grabbed her purse and her coat and walked out of the courthouse and the meeting was adjourned, just like that.

Two days later after forfeiting and losing out on the grant, we all attended our regular monthly council meeting. The lady who had voted "No" on the application did not attend, which did not make a quorum so an executive meeting was called.

Going over the grant application as a team, we noticed a small clause amendment which ABC had included directly in the middle of the fifteen-page application. An amendment that had been added to the contract which none of us had even noticed. The amendment read:

> "The City is being given a grant in the amount of 35,000 (which is being lowered from the initial $50,000 we usually allot). If the $45,000 is not spent or allotted out by the community within five days of receiving this grant, the city will forfeit the grant and will be penalized at a rate of 35% to be spread out over three years starting the following month of forfeiting to be paid directly to ABC, and the city will not be eligible to receive future fundings."

If not allotted out or spent within five days, what? We usually hold on to the funds until the next council meeting which could be well over a week or two from now!

Sitting around the council tables we all looked at each other in total surprise wondering what would have happened to or meant for the entire community if we had voted "Yes to receive this grant?" The mayor spoke for a minute and said, "We would have made a major, major mistake."

If not for that one lady who had thoroughly read over all fifteen pages carefully and caught that one small added amendment and held up the vote, our whole community would have been in a whole lot of trouble. We would have suffered greatly and been in deep debt for many years to come which we did not need.

At the next council meeting, everyone including citizens and the council members apologized to her for their behavior and the way they had treated her.

She was thanked and applauded by the whole community because she stood alone against the crowd even against me. I looked over to her across the council chambers and simply smiled and she smiled back. She had tears in her eyes, but these were tears of joy. My dear reader, you may be out numbered but you have a voice.

As a true vessel for Christ my dear reader there are going to be many times throughout your life when you are going to have to stand alone even against a crowd. Jesus stood alone many times even when it came to His disciples.

The Bible gives many examples where individuals had to stand alone. Take for example:

* David, he stood alone against the giant Goliath, *"Thou comest with a sword, and with a spear, and with a shield: but I come to thee in the name of the Lord of host" (1 Samuel 17:45 KJV).*
* Moses stood alone in Pharaohs in courts in his attempt to free the Hebrew slaves from bondage, *"And the Lord spake unto Moses, Go unto Pharaoh, and say unto him, thus saith the Lord, Let my people go, that they may serve me"* (Exodus 8:1 KJV).
* Shadrach, Meshach and Abednego stood alone facing the fiery furnace with their refusal to bow down to king Nebuchadnezzar stating, *"We are not careful to answer thee in this matter. If it be so, our God whom we serve is able to deliver us from the burning fiery furnace"* (Dan. 3:16-17 KJV).

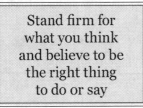

Stand firm for what you think and believe to be the right thing to do or say

* Rahab stood alone by hiding spies from danger in her attic while they searched out the land of Jericho, *"And the king of Jericho sent unto Rahab, saying, Bring forth the men that are come to thee, which are entered into thine house and the woman took the two men and hid them"* (Joshua 2:3-4 KJV).

Standing alone is not a sign of fear but is courageous. It takes courage to stand alone and you will eventually find out that when you follow the crowd you can't get no further than the crowd, you have actually set limits on yourself.

You may be right or you may be wrong standing alone but be courageous in what you decide to do. You have a voice, you may be out numbered but you have a voice. You may lose friends but you have a voice. Use the voice God gave you and more importantly stand firm for what you think and believe is the right thing to do or say.

BEING ALONE

Being alone and being lonely are two different things. Being alone means that you are separate from others while loneliness is a feeling. You can experience being alone just by sitting in a room by yourself and on the other hand experience loneliness being by yourself in the midst of a crowd.

But regarding, "Being Alone." Sometimes it is going to require you to go or do things, alone, going against the grain or you may choose to separate yourself from others just to get a piece of mind or to think things over without being harassed, pressured or influenced by others. I will list a few instances when solitude or being alone might be necessary:

1. **Time to recharge after a stressful day**

   When Jesus 12 disciples returned from ministry, He advised them to separate themselves from the crowd that were following them so they could rest and recharge (Mark 6:30-32 kjv). After a hard day's work dealing with numerous people, it is a good feeling to finally get away from everything and everybody because you simply want to be alone for a little while, nothing wrong with that at all.

2. **Before making important decisions**

   Jesus in His early ministry spent the previous whole night alone in prayer before making the decision of whom He would to choose as His 12 disciples (Luke 6:12-13 kjv). There were times when I have been pressured by people to make impulsive decisions but at the very last minute, I decided that my wife and I needed more time to think things over. This allowed us time to get away from the pressure of hungry sales people to pray on it first allowing God to give His insight.

3. <u>To work through times of grief and distress</u>

When Jesus had learned that His cousin John the Baptist had been beheaded, He went away to be by Himself to grieve, (read Matt. 14:14 kjv).

Several years ago after my Father died, and being consoled by so many, I only found a piece of mind by being alone sitting in my prayer closet, my secret place where I could talk privately with The Lord.

I needed time to pray and to come to the realization of not seeing my him again. But even then, I had to give God praise for fifty- three years of being with him because if I would have lost sight of God, I would have been totally lost.

Recovering from heartbreaking grief is a time when being alone will probably be the most helpful to you, well it was for me. Surrounded by so many people, so much noise and confusion, solitude may be your only means of comfort.

Believe me, there are going to be times in your life when you are going to have say, "I need to be alone if you don't mind." Now, that is not being nasty nor is it being inconsiderate of others, it simply says in a nice way, "I need to get away from yall so I can think and get a piece of mind."

ACTING ALONE

Several years ago, a small child fell down a well fifteen feet deep that was too narrow for anyone to simply climb down into it to rescue the child. The situation went on for hours and eventually into the darkness of night.

Soon a head rescuer arrived and made a suggestion of digging a hole fifteen feet away from the well, straight down then across to where the child had fallen as a rescue attempt. But by the well being so close to a creek many felt the well would flood drowning both the child and the rescuer, so that suggestion failed. Another suggested sending down a rope for the child to grab a hold on to, but the well was too narrow.

After all suggestions had been made and everyone was scratching their heads, a tall slender man came from out of nowhere and quietly walked to the front of the crowd and said, "I will go down into the well and get the child."

There was complete silence while the slim man lassoed a rope around his shoulders and tied the other side to a tree and slowly lowered himself down the well. *"Be fearless, you are never alone" (Joshua 1:9 kjv).*

With one tug from the bottom of the well, he was pulled up to the top of the well with the child wrapped around his body. The child dehydrated and dirty but was not harmed was quickly rushed to a nearby hospital. The slender man dirty and totally exhausted not saying a word simply walked away from the news reporters and the huge crowd sat by himself against a tree.

The next morning a nationwide news reporter caught up with the slender man and asked him, "Do you know that you are a national hero, but why did you choose to do what you did?" He simply answered, "I listened to all the suggestions on how they were going to rescue that little child and when no solution was made, I knew in my heart that I was the one who had to go down into the well and rescue the little child and I had to do it alone." After that report, the tall slender man simply walked away and was never seen again.

We read of many instances in the Bible where servants of God either went alone or had to deal with various situations, alone. Take for example: Job, he lost everything, His family, wealth, he almost lost his life but, he had to deal with the struggles from Satin alone without any help of friends, even without the help from his own wife.

Take for example David, he had to deal with the torment from a jealous King Saul all alone who for years tried to kill him. David was so successful on the missions Saul sent him on that the people started singing: "Saul hath slain his thousands, and David his ten thousands" (1 Samuel 18:7).

Saul was the king yet his people were praising David instead of him. Saul's jealousy grew to the point to where he actually tried to kill David more than once (1 Samuel 18:10-11).

But David said to Saul, "Why do you listen when men say 'David is bent on harming you'? This day you have seen with your own eyes how the Lord delivered you into my hands in the cave. Some urged me to kill you, but I 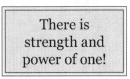 spared you; I said, I will not lift my hand against my master, because he is the Lord's anointed" (1 Samuel 24:9 NIV), David knew where his strength came from.

There is strength and power of one. There will be times when you will either have to be alone, go alone or act alone but these will be the times when your courage will take front seat and more importantly your faith in God will be tested.

Even our Lord Jesus Christ had to either stand alone or act alone on many occasions. Yes, Jesus had a team of twelve and some very close friends but, there were on so many occasions where He felt that He needed to act alone or simply needed to be alone. Let's talk about a few instances where Jesus was in need of solitude:

You remember when the disciples went into the city of Samaria to get food and left Jesus alone. He had a conversation with the Samaritan woman at Jacob's well (John 4 kjv). The conversation 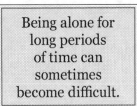 between the two led to her receiving spiritual wisdom and knowledge from Jesus. But, He had to be alone with her for this to take place because of the different cultural beliefs at that time.

What about the time when Jesus went out to a mountain side to pray, and spent the night praying. When morning came, He called His disciples to Him (Luke: 6:12-13 kjv) and among them He chose twelve, whom He also named Apostles. It was important for Jesus to be alone during this time so that He could have a one-on-one peaceful conversation with His Father.

But I have to admit something to you my dear reader and that is being alone for long periods of time especially for me can sometimes become difficult giving my mind and conscious extra time to wonder off into areas where normally I would rather choose not to go. Sometimes I have to catch myself and bring myself back to reality.

It is easy to get discouraged and to be tempted especially when you are alone or finding yourself in solitude for extended periods of time.

Do you remember the time when Jesus went alone into the desert and fasted for forty days? He was tired and more than likely hungry which is probably the worst time for one to be alone more or less to be tempted by someone.

Now, here comes Satin asking Jesus all these tempting questions like, *"I thou be the Son of God, command that these stones be made bread"* which we all know that Jesus would have no problem in doing but Jesus refused to be tempted by responding, "Man shall not live by bread alone, but by every word that proceeded out of the mouth of God" (Matthew 4:1-4 kjv).

And after that, Satin took Jesus up into the holy city, saying, "Well, if thou be the Son of God, cast thyself down: for it is written, He shall give His angels charge concerning thee: and in their hands they shall bear thee up, lest at any time thou dash thy foot against a stone" (Matthew 4:5-6 kjv). Here you can see how the devil is trying to use Jesus own words against Him.

But Jesus simply responds by saying, "It is also written again, Thou shalt not tempt the Lord thy God" (vs 7). Jesus even being weak, tired and being tempted knew how to respond back at the right time with the WORDS of God! Question is, would you know how to react when you are alone and being tempted?

My beloved, I want you to remember this. Anything, including temptations and periods of loneliness or anything that can put in you in a position to where your worship, your peace or your joy can being disturbed, remember that there is an inward Power working within you that will allow you to raise your hands and give God the glory as though those things don't even exist, it's called the power of the

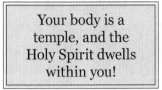

Your body is a temple, and the Holy Spirit dwells within you!

Holy Spirit! Oh, "Know ye not that ye are the temple of God, and that the Spirit of God dwelleth in you?"(1 Cor. 3:16 kjv) Yes, your body is a temple, and the Holy Spirit dwells within you. The Holy Spirit is powerful and will give you strength!

> *"But ye shall receive power, after that the Holy Ghost is come upon you: and ye shall be witnesses unto me both in Jerusalem and in all Judaea, and in Samaria, and unto the uttermost part of the earth" (Acts 1:8 kjv).*

GOING ALONE

I was taught a valuable lesson as a teenager growing up and that was, never take your friend to an interview that was only meant for you. I was advised that a seasonal job was available at this company where my Dad was getting our television fixed. Summer break had just started and I was in desperate need to spend and give away money that was burning a hole in my pockets.

The job did not start until the beginning of the week so I had enough time to prepare at least two days. Made sure clock was set to wake me up at 9am, clothes set out and hair cut to perfection, I was ready. I was so excited about my new job to come that I had to share the good news with one of my best friends, John. I told him the place, time I was to start and what I was going to wear. He was so happy for me.

Monday morning came and I sat on the porch waiting for my Dad to come out of the house to take me to the interview which took him an extra forty-five minutes, yep, we were going to be late. As I sat on the porch, I noticed my friend John and his parents driving pass our house, he waved and I waved back. Such a good friend he was probably praying that I would get the new job.

When we arrived for the interview, the hiring person said that the position had been filled. I was so upset mainly at my Dad because we were late for the interview. The next day, I called John to see if he wanted to go to the park to shoot some ball. He said that he had work to do. I'm thinking probably more yardwork or some chores his Mom had prepared for him.

With nothing to do, I again sat on the porch. Here comes John walking down the street dressed in the uniform for the company where I was supposed to be working. I looked at him and I asked, "What are you doing, where are you going? I was supposed to be working there." John

> Remember, Jesus went alone on many occasions

simply said, "Well, since the job was open, I thought that I would apply for it too and they hired me on the spot."

At that very moment I did not care about the job, I just looked at him with a big smile wanting to rip that uniform off of him and put it on me. Yes, I felt betrayed, Yes, I felt terribly angry for a while but one thing my Dad taught me and I learned from the whole situation is that there are going to be times in life requiring you to go alone! Remember, Jesus went alone on many occasions and simply needed solitude and there will be times when you my dear reader will also have to go alone.

Reflection and Relevant Questions

1. Why do you feel that it is easier to compromise and go along with the majority as opposed to standing alone with your own ideas and opinion?
2. Describe a time in your life when you supported an idea that no one else supported and you had to stand alone.
3. Isolation and loneliness are a few areas of Being alone. Give a few examples of how you overcame those feelings when you were alone.

11

»»»»»»» ««««««««

INTENSE RELATIONSHIP
WITH CHRIST

Draw nigh to God, and He will draw nigh
to you. Cleanse your hands, ye sinners;
and purify your hearts, ye double minded.
Wash your hands, you sinners; purify your
hearts, for your loyalty is divided between
God and the world," (James 4:8 kjv).

ave you ever been so in love with something or
someone to the point to where you can't sleep, can't
think and you can't do anything else but think about
that particular thing or person? That is what it feels
like to have that personal relationship with Christ. That is what it feels
like when you have made up your mind to follow Christ, to serve Him
and to be filled with the Holy Spirit.

Do you want to receive the Holy Spirit? A love that surpasses all
understanding? My beloved, it is a love that never fails and one that
we all long for and desire to have. Do you want and desire that kind
of love? Do you have a hole in your heart that has been empty for so
long that it is in need of mending?

I'm here to tell you that God has a blessing with your name on it and He can supply all your needs and wants and is able to fill that empty hole. It's all involved with you having a relationship with Him.

You need to develop a relationship with Him, a relationship to where it becomes emotional (*you find yourself crying and weeping for no reason*) allowing you to encounter His presence and experience the working of the Holy Ghost! Now that you know, do you still want and desire a closer relationship with Christ, ok, then let's get it!

ENCOUNTERING GOD'S PRESENCE

People have often asked me the questions, "What does it feel like or how do you know when you are in the presence of The Lord?" or "How will I know when the Holy Spirit has come upon me?" Well, I can only speak from my personal experiences such as me feeling like someone is present greater than myself working on situations for my betterment or a feeling of strength will come upon me to handle a difficult situation.

Many times when I am in the presence of God, a sudden chill will run across my arms or a specific sensational feeling letting me know that I am surrounded by His presence.

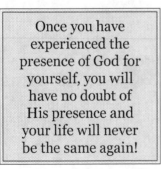

Once you have experienced the presence of God for yourself, you will have no doubt of His presence and your life will never be the same again!

To tell you the truth, there is a sense of peace and rest when you enter into God's presence. Once you have experienced the presence of God for yourself, you will have no doubt of His presence and your life will never be the same again. I can be sitting on the couch, I can be riding in the car and His presence can fall upon me, but I feel His presence mostly when I am praying and crying out to the Lord with expectations.

One thing is for sure though, that is, you will never experience The Lord's presence or the Lord's love in your heart until you first invite Him into it! It is not proper to show up at functions or gatherings unless you are invited. The Lord is not going to show up unless He is received. Once you receive and invite the Lord into your heart, you will experience a love more deeper than you can imagine and the fullness and glory of His presence but, first you must, invite Him into your heart.

But you may still ask, "How do I myself actually know when the good Lord is present and He is alive and is working or attempting to speak to me?" "How do I have an encounter with God", "My friend, I can only tell you this, it comes with having a personal relationship with The Lord. First, ask The Lord to forgive you of your sins and then surrender your life to Him. Ask God to come into your heart and fill you with the Holy Spirit and God will begin to speak to you in so many ways."

Let me give you several Biblical signs that God is alive and how He speaks and works on your behalf, for example:

1. <u>He speaks to you through His word.</u> (2 Tim 3:16 kjv)
2. <u>He speaks audibly to you (Acts 9:4-7 kjv)</u>
    You remember God spoke to Saul audibly while he was on his way to Damascus.
3. <u>He speaks to you through other people (Exodus 18:14-17 kjv)</u>
    You remember God spoke through Moses to speak to Israel *people are put in positions to help you get to a higher level
4. <u>He speaks to you through dreams and visions (Acts 18:19 kjv)</u>
    You remember God Spoke through Joseph's dreams
5. <u>He speaks to you through your prayers (Psalms 66:17, 66:20 kjv)</u>
    You remember God spoke through Hannah while she was praying for a child
6. <u>He speaks to you when certain verses keep coming up</u>

When you begin to develop a relationship with Christ, He will begin speaking to you and You will recognize His voice. In all actuality, God speaks to you every day, and wants to reveal to you your position in Christ with Him. The question is, are you listening and paying attention?

EXPERIENCE WITH THE HOLY SPIRIT

The land of Samaria had been suffering from extreme famine and

God speaks to you every day, are you listening?

drought for three years (according to James 5:17 kjv)mainly because of wicked King Ahab's rejection of God. King Ahab and people of the land cried out day and night to their false god Baal to send the rain to no avail.

Elijah went up to the top of Mt. Carmel and he cast himself down upon the earth, and put his face between his knees(1 Kings 18:42 kjv). Question, why did Elijah put his face between his knees? First, this shows humility and secondly, to close out all outside influences while praying so that he could concentrate and focus on hearing clearly what God was speaking to him.

Until you can clearly hear what the Holy Spirit is saying to you, you will never know the full details of what God has for you. But, how can you clearly hear the Holy Spirit speaking to you in the midst of confusion, in the midst of doubters or you find yourself going against everything the world is saying.

Sometimes you just need a quiet place or to be like Elijah and simply put your head between your knees to close out unfamiliar voices and the world *"And be not conformed to this world: but be ye transformed by the renewing of your mind, that ye may prove what is that good, acceptable, and perfect will of God"* (Romans 12:2 kjv). If you think about it, the life you are living right now is the direct result of voices you heard and listened to in the past.

You have so many people talking, so many voices coming in from all different directions and if you listen to them all, you will miss out and get what the Holy Spirit is saying to you all wrong. This is why you have to know the Holy Spirits voice on a deeper level more than merely just another spirit.

The Holy Spirit is a person, a divine person. The Holy Spirit has power, divine power. The Holy Spirit has energy, divine energy. The Holy Spirit is a Divine Spirit that we must know personally and be filled with! Knowing the Holy Spirit is like having a close friend, one you can talk to and listen to. One who can guide and prompt you to do things that are in accordance with God.

In His last message in the book of John, Jesus refers to the Holy Spirit as if a close personal friend or companion:

> "But the Comforter, which is the Holy Ghost, whom the Father will send in my name, he shall teach you all things, and bring all things to your remembrance, whatsoever I have said unto you" (John 14:26 kjv).

Apostle Paul encourages us to be filled with the Holy Spirit:

> "And be not drunk with wine, but be filled with the Holy Spirit." (Ephesians 5:18 kjv)

My dear reader it is of upmost importance that you develop a personal relationship with the Holy Spirit and with God so that you will know what He has for you that you may enjoy them. As I mentioned earlier the Holy Spirit will give you energy, energy to face the enemy head on and power to defeat them!

> The Holy Spirit will give you energy!

Whether you cry out between your knees or standing upright, listen to what the spirit is saying and allow the Holy Spirit to fill your heart and soul. He is right there waiting for you to open up your heart to let him in.

Reflection and Relevant Questions

1. Tell about a time when you had an encounter with the Holy Spirit that you have only kept to yourself? Explain.
2. What are some signs that God is present in your life today?
    a. In what ways are you developing a personal relationship with Christ?
3. Do you believe that God has a greater plan for your life? Explain.

12

》》》》》》》《《《《《《《《

JUST JESUS

*Now therefore, I pray thee, if I have found grace
in thy sight, shew me now thy way, that I may
know thee, that I may find grace in thy sight:
and consider that this nation is thy people.*
(Exodus 33:3 kjv)

s Thomas Watson patiently listened, some of the most famous words in history finally came through "Watson Come here." These were the first intelligible words and voice he heard spoken over the telephone by its inventor Alexander Graham Bell in 1876. What a thrill of excitement it must have been to hear those words after years and years of trial and error for Watson to finally hear a voice, a sound, anything to come through the lines.

I am sure that Bell had no idea that over two hundred years later his invention would lead to citizens speaking through cellular towers. The excitement was not so much in completing his work, the excitement came from finally hearing Alexanders Graham Bell's voice.

What excitement it is to finally hear the voice of someone you have not heard from in years. You have possible been thinking about them a lot and have even made plans to call them but never got around to doing it.

To hear the voice of the Lord is different from the anticipation and excitement of hearing from a relative or a friend. While you are waiting to hear from them, the Lord's voice can sometimes come instantly.

The Bible says:

> "Call unto me, and I will answer thee, and show thee
> great and mighty things"(Jeremiah 33:3 kjv).

But what does it actually mean to hear the voice of the Lord? Hearing from the Lord my dear reader first of all it requires listening, patience and at times, prayer. How can you possibly get a word from the Lord without first listening and being able to distinguish His voice from outside distractions.

Secondly, you must be patient. This is most important especially when praying. You may have been asking God for answers for a while and each time it seems like He is not hearing you. And to tell you the truth, some prayers are not answered immediately for a couple reasons. One reason you don't see more prayers being answered is that so many of us basically deny Christ by our actions all week. You have not spent time with Christ but you call Him friend. You don't even acknowledge that you know Him, but when Sunday comes around you are ready to hear a prophetic word from Him.

"My sheep hear my voice, and I know them, and they follow me" (John 10:27 kjv)

How can you really expect to hear from the Lord if you don't spend time or even acknowledge Him?

And along with that, it's going to take a little patience in hearing from the Lord. He knows our future and when you decide to go out on the limb alone, it can be devastating.

Many of us maybe even you have been patiently waiting to hear a Word, worried about so many things when there is only one thing required for us to do and that is: to sit at the feet of Jesus and wait on Him. Anything you ask of God, He will give it. Jesus said:

> "I am the resurrection, and the life: he that believeth in me, though he were dead, yet shall he live: And whosoever liveth and believeth in me shall never die" (John 11:25-26 kjv).

You may even be in the most peaceful atmosphere waiting patiently on hearing from the Lord and still things seem to be going nowhere, it will simply require more from you.

These are the times when you have no other choice but to cry out to the Lord in prayer: *"Father, I need more of You, just tell me what I need to do and I promise I will do it."* To get exactly what you are seeking, to hear His voice audibly many times will require a sincere prayer of faith. Remember that delay does not always mean denial. The Lord does things in His perfect timing that will be beneficial to you.

Do you believe that Jesus is the Son of God? Do you believe that Jesus died on the cross for your sins? Do you believe that He also rose again on the third day? If you said, "Yes", you have an everlasting life in Christ Jesus! He hears you crying at night alone and your prayers out of desperation and they will not go unanswered!

The Lord is never going to ignore you or your petition, in fact He is constantly speaking to you. It is a communication similar to that of a radio transmitter. Just like you need to get on the right wave frequency to get a good signal, you need to get on the right spiritual wave frequency to open up the lines between the Lord and yourself.

You need to check your heavenly wave signal on a daily basis and make sure nothing is obstructing your communication with the Lord because if the connection is not met, the power from above or anything you are looking for, will not be met. The Lord is speaking, Can you hear Him? A relationship with Christ requires open communication.

WHAT'S IN A NAME?

People call you based on the season they knew you. If someone knew you as the water boy in high school but now you are playing in the NBA, don't be offended when they yell out to you, "Hey water boy" because that is who they knew you as during that particular season when that was who you were. But that is not your name just a reference. They might have yelled out your name by another name if they knew you were playing in the NBA. That's why you have to be careful how you treat people. Just because they were one way during a certain time in their life does not mean that they are the same person later on in their life, names stay the same but people change.

But what's in a name? People will carry a professional football teams name on the back of their jersey indicating their affiliation with that team. A person will wave banners with another person's name on it indicating their support of them. But, why is a name so important? What is in a good name? Why is your name so important?

My name is Paul Phillips, what's the big deal? I'll tell you what the big deal is. Let me tell you about a time when that name carried big weight. When I was maybe eleven or twelve years of age, my Dad dropped me off at a local barbers shop (I mentioned this in one of my previous books) and said that he would pick me up in about a half hour. When I walked in the barber shop, I found myself in the midst of about ten or fifteen grown men but anyway I went to sit down.

Not long afterwards, a barber came up to me and asked who I was and I said my name is, Paul Phillips. He looked at me with a half grin and smiling at the same time. He went back over to his chair and spoke to some of the other guys and they all looked at me at the same time and I have to admit I was a little afraid thinking "Daddy, where are you at?" Hey, I was only six or seven. Then another guy yelled out, "Hey yall this is Paul Phillips son sitting here!"

And just like that every gentlemen in the shop got up out of their chairs, came over to me and they began to introduce themselves to me. I even stood up shaking their hands as if I was popular or I had done something great, but it was not about me, it was about my Dad and the reputation that he had made for himself with these guys over the past years.

Several of the men had mentioned that they had worked with my Dad for many years and were good friends while others were members of the same lodge my Dad belonged to and all this change of attitudes among everyone towards me was simply because of the mentioning of a name. When I mentioned the name Paul Phillips, the atmosphere and the men's attitude towards me changed and I had done absolutely nothing except mentioning a name. That good name going before me carried benefits: I was

> A Good name is rather to be chosen than great riches, and loving favor than silver and gold.
> Proverbs 22:1 KJV

put in front of everyone to get my haircut, a free haircut I must say, more than anything else, I was made to feel special!

Now, please understand something, my Dad was not famous by any means, never played sports, not head of a major company, but, the way he carried himself said it all. For example, he never shook another man's hands siting down. He always greeted a man first by shaking hands then talking.

He always took care of our family and it was customary for visitors or family members coming from out of state for him to say to them, "If you can make it across the Ohio boarder traveling to get here, you have a place to stay" or "Your money is no good in Ohio" meaning that he was going to pay for whatever they desired or wanted, they did not have to spend a dime while staying with us. To say "Your money is no good here in Ohio" to someone is one hospitality that I am still working on, please forgive me.

There's something about that name, Jesus

Getting back to the topic, "What's in a name?" Let's think about the time when Jesus was speaking to His Disciples:

> Jesus saith unto His disciples, "Whom do men say that I am?" And they said, "Some say that thou art John the Baptist: some Elias; and others, Jeremias, or one of the prophets."

He saith unto them, "But whom say ye that I am?"
And Simon Peter answered and said, "Thou art the
Christ, the Son of the living God."
Matthew 16:13-16 KJV

Why do you think Jesus asked his disciples the question, *"But whom say ye that I am?"* Considering the fact that they were always around Jesus, they sat and had supper with Him and had many private talks with Jesus, so why did He ask them that question?

> Why do you think Jesus asked his disciples the question, "But whom say ye that I am?"

Was it really that important that they knew that He was on a higher spiritual level than the prophets and disciples and not just another prophet?

Of course it was that important! They knew and we need to know the importance in knowing Jesus Christ, the Great I am, our Lord and Savior intimately and on a more personal level!

In the gospel of John, Jesus repeats the words "I am" seven times so that we all may see His full character.

I AM:

The Bread of life

And Jesus said to them, "I am the bread of life.
He who comes to me shall never hunger, and he who
believes in me shall never thirst." John 6:35 NKJV

Light of the World

Then Jesus spoke to them again saying, "I am the
light of the world. He who follows me shall not walk in
darkness, but have the light of life." John 8:12 NKJV

The Door

"I am the door. If anyone enters by Me, he will be saved, and will go in and out and find pasture." John 10:9 ESV

The Good Shepherd

"I am the good shepherd. The good shepherd gives his life for his sheep." John 10:11 NKJV

The Resurrection and the Life

"I am the resurrection and the life. He who believes in Me, though he may die, he shall live. And whosoever lives and believes in Me shall never die." John 11:25-26 NKJV

The Way, the Truth and the Life

"I am the way, the truth, and the life. No one comes to the Father except through Me." John 14:6 NKJV

The Vine

"I am the vine, you are the branches. He who abides in Me, and I in him, bears much fruit; for without Me you can do nothing." John 15:5 NKJV

"I am" is in the present tense. Jesus did not say "I will" neither did He say, "I might" He said, "I am" meaning that He is in the present tense and is presently in your life at this present moment! Regarding His disciples, it was as simple as this, Jesus wanted to make sure that His disciples knew for a fact that He was the Son of the living God and that when they were out in the public sector all by themselves, they needed to know who they were representing, Jesus Christ, the Son of the living God!

You, yourself are a representative of Jesus Christ as well. Each time you step out the front door, you are a representative 0f Jesus Christ, when you walk into the office, you are a representative 0f Jesus Christ, when you speak, you are representing Jesus Christ.

If you are to be a follower and a vessel for Christ it should be clear who you represent. There should be no doubt or compromise when it comes to the Word or Jesus Christ! If you have a struggle believing God, then you will have a struggle submitting to His Will.

But, let's take a moment and talk about the name "JESUS." The name JESUS is the most distinctive, most powerful name known by people all around the world more than any other name. It is the one name that can't be forged and spoken in over six thousand languages and still be understood by all. The name "Jesus" is more than just a name. The name of Jesus brings us comfort in life and death and hope in this hopeless world.

> The Name JESUS is a Name known by people all around the world more than any other Name!

There is power and authority in the name of JESUS! Here are a couple facts about that particular name:

1. There is no other name under the sun given to us whereby we can be saved (read Acts 4:12).
2. When you believe in Jesus Christ, you have life in His name (read John 20:31).

But let me stop right there and clarify just one thing. The name of Jesus is not some kind of magical wand you can wave that will give you authority and power. No, The Power in the name, comes from the person behind the name, JESUS!

POWER IN THE NAME

Yes, there is power in the name of Jesus especially when He is on your side. No matter how big your battle may be, no matter how big the struggles get in your life, just mention the name and the battle field will change! The name of Jesus carries weight!

Take for instance the small boy David when he went up against a huge undefeated Philistine giant named Goliath. Now, Goliath had defeated the Israeli army and he was ready for his next challenge and here comes little David:

> "And when the Philistine (Goliath) looked about, and saw David, he disdained hm: for he was but a youth, and of a fair countenance. And the Philistine said unto David, come to me, and I will give thy flesh unto the fowls of the air, and to the beast of the field (1Samuel 17:42-43 KJV).

Then David said to the Philistine, "You come to me with a sword, with a spear, and with a javelin. But I come to you in the <u>name of the LORD of Host</u>, the God of the armies of Israel, whom thou hast defied"(I Samuel 17:45 kjv). David took out his sling shot and with one rock, he hit Goliath and the battle was over just like that. Meaning that, no matter how big, how strong, or how prepared Goliath was, when

But I come to thee in the name of the LORD!! 1 Sam. 17:45

David had God on his side, Goliath did not have a fighting chance of winning.

My dear reader, if anyone ever want to down you for who you are, you tell them just like David told Goliath, "You came at me with a sword but I defeated you with a rock, you came at me with a shield but I defeated you with a rock." You have to stand on what you have and what know, the Word of God! "David smote Goliath in his forehead; and he fell upon his face to the earth"(1 Sam 17:49 kjv) and the battle was over before it even started. It does not matter who you are, a Giant, a Pastor, a Billionaire or even the President of the USA. The Bible says that:

> "At the name of JESUS, every knee should bow, of things in heaven, and things in earth, and things under the earth; And that every tongue should confess that Jesus Christ is Lord, to the glory of God the Father" (Philippians 2:10-11 kjv).

No one is above the name of Jesus! When the name of Jesus is mentioned or spoken, the whole story changes and that is why we must know who HE is and who we represent.

JESUS, YOU MAKE THE DARKNESS TREMBLE!
JESUS, YOU MAKE THE WINDS TO CEASE!
JESUS, YOU MAKE THE SUN TO SHINE!
Jesus You are King of Kings and Lord of Lords!

LIGHT

Let's suppose you were in a huge auditorium and suddenly the lights were turned off and in an instant you found yourself in complete darkness, what would be your first instinct? To look for the closest light switch I would think but what if you could not find one.

But, against a far wall there was a small hole about the size of a quarter where a slight inkling of light was seeping through, what would you do? Run towards it of course. Why is that? Why run towards the small inkling of light when you were surrounded by a huge auditorium of darkness?

Thing is, that small inkling of light was a sign of hope, a sign to possibly finding more light which would allow you to use your eyes to see.

> The light of the world is the Son of God, Jesus

When light enters our eyes it signals to the brain which allows us to decipher an objects location, movement and distance. Light, light makes it possible for us to see the different colors in a spectrum. Light gives us a better chance of avoiding possible danger. Bottom line is that without light we would have no sight or vision.

Light is the fastest thing in the universe. Have you ever thought as to why you see lightning before you actually hear the thunder or you can see the smoke of the gun shot indicating the start of a race before you actually hear the sound of it? Well, the light of it travels faster than the sound of it which is why you see things a lot of times before you hear the effects of it. But in all this quickness of light, God moves on our behalf, even faster!

Light, was the first thing God created before the sun, the moon and the stars, before the seas and even before He created man in His own image. When we think even of the powerful and greatness of the mighty sun, still it is not, "The light of the world." The light of the world is the Son of God, Jesus.

Jesus refers to Himself as "I am the light of the world: he that followeth me shall not walk in darkness, but shall have the light of life"(John 8:12 kjv).

Yes, my dear reader, Jesus is the only light we need to follow Him especially today in our daily lives. He says, *"I, the LORD have called thee in righteousness, and will hold thine hand, and will keep thee, and give thee for a covenant of the people, for a light of the Gentiles"(*Isaiah 42:6 kjv).

My dear reader, you may be going through a season in your life right now where you feel stuck in darkness, you feel that you are surrounded by darkness and you just need one small inkling of light, just one small feeling of hope, any little sign that would put the long-lost smile back on your face.

The hope you are looking for, the light you are looking for at the end of the tunnel you will find only in Jesus Christ. He is our hope and our light in this dying world.

The Bible says that "God is light and in Him is no darkness" (1 John 1:5 kjv). While we seem to try our hardest in fulfilling dark spaces in our heart but we always seem to end up in the same place where we started.

In order to be an overcoming vessel for Christ we must learn to put our trust in God and stop living in routine. Stop spending so much of your day doing the same things and try applying more time with God especially in praying:

> "But thou, when thou prayest, enter into thy closet, and when thou hast shut the door, pray to thy Father which is in secret; and thy Father which seeth in secret shall reward thee openly" (Matthew 6:6 kjv).

As you can see, light is something very special especially the light of Jesus. The Bible says: "Let your light so shine before men, that they may see your good works, and glorify your Father which is in heaven"(Matthew 5:16).

He wants you to live life like He intended. He desires for you to be a shining light to those around you. The light of God will attract and draw you and others towards Him each and every time.

Reflection and Relevant Questions

1. Paul begins section two of this chapter with this: *"What is in a name? What is in a good name? Why is your name so important?"* Explain
   a. In what ways can having a good name be more valuable or beneficial to you than riches like silver and gold? Read proverbs 22:1

2. Can you remember a time in your life when someone else's good name or their good reputation proceeded you and you benefited from it?
3. Why do you think LIGHT (spiritually and physically) is so important in our lives?

13

»»»»»»» «««««««

BE READY!

Therefore be ye also ready: for in such an hour
as ye think not the son of man cometh
Matthew 24:44

remember reading about the Revolutionary War
(1775-1783) in high school. During the Revolutionary
War, there was a group of men known as the Minute
Men. This group of men usually comprised of self-
trained civilian colonist known for being ready and prepared to
fight at a minutes notice when there arose a threat of war against
the colonies.

I once worked as a firefighter for our community. It was a small
community only a mile in diameter. Even though the community
was considered a bit smaller than neighboring communities we still
had our share of building and house fires. I could be called upon any
time of the day to fight a fire.

Whatever the case was, I could be sleeping, driving or out to
dinner, I had to stop what I was doing and speed to the firehouse,
put on my boots, jacket, oxygen tank and jump on the back of the
firetruck hoping it had not taken off without me. Believe me it is hard
to jump on a moving firetruck with a hundred-pound firefighting
equipment scraped on your back.

Minutemen, Firefighters are different in many ways but one thing they both have in common is that: They both have to always Be Ready for action at a minutes notice!

> It reminds us that we should always be Prepared and on High Alert and Watchful for the soon Coming of the Lord.

The Bible gives a great illustration of how we should always be ready and always on alert:

Now, there were ten virgins (perhaps at a wedding banquet) each carrying a lamp all waiting for their bridegroom to come which they expected to arrive sometimes during the night.

Five of the virgins were wise and had prepared oil in their lamps and five virgins who were foolish who did not have any oil for their lamps. When it was announced in the middle of the night the foolish begged for oil for their lamps and asked the wise for oil. The wise only had enough oil for themselves so when the foolish virgins went out to buy oil they missed the groom and no matter how hard they cried, "Lord, Lord open the door for us to enter" they were locked out of the banquet. Jesus said, "Watch, therefore, for ye know neither the day nor the hour wherein the Son of man cometh" (Matthew 25:1-13 kjv).

It reminds us that we should always be prepared and on high alert and watchful for the soon coming of the Lord because we just don't know when He is coming back again. When Jesus spoke of His return, He spoke in terms of "soon" not as immediately but that He would come back which could happen at any moment.

> "Watch ye therefore: for ye know not when
> the master of the house cometh, at even,
> or at midnight, or at the cockcrowing, or
> in the morning" (Mark 13:35 kjv).

So how do we as Christians properly prepare ourselves to always be ready and on high alert? Is it even possible to be ready at all times sharing words of advice to someone if we don't know or have scriptures to back it up? Do you even feel that you know enough or confident enough to talk about the Bible? Believe me when I tell you, that you do know enough to talk about the Bible, you just need a little confidence in yourself and you need to read the manual, I mean reading the Holy Bible more, that's all, it's never too late or you too old to start. Jesus simply says, "So always be ready" (Matthew 24:42 NCV).

NEVER TOO OLD TO LEARN

Let me tell you something I learned from my nine-year-old grandson Jon Jon who came to visit my wife and I over the summer. Now remember, I have been to college, I read my Bible every day, graduated from a Bible School and have been Ordained as a Minister, I should know a little something.

Yeah, I was one of those kids who thought they should have left their parent's home at ten because at the time I felt I knew everything, yeah right!

Here I go, times had been tough for my wife and myself the past couple of years or so and we decided to drop our cable service and just use the internet service which many people are doing these days.

But, I will to this day complain to my wife that I love to watch sports on television and that I have not seen a live professional basketball, baseball or football game on my big screen television in over five years and this is the truth. I had gotten so tired and bored from watching rerun internet shows and movies all day, I NEEDED MY LIVE SPORTS!

Well, my Grandson Jon Jon came to visit and would you know it, my television disappointments and frustrations spilled out upon to him. From his knowledge from back home (they have cable) and reading my television manual and looking at my frustrations he said, "PaPa, you know

> I guess that I am not as smart as I thought I was!

that you can watch live sports on your big screen television screaming from your cell phone." I looked at him and said just one word, "Ha?"

The look on my face was as if he had just discovered a cure for a worldwide epidemic. I said, "Jon Jon, what do you mean?" He showed me and instantly there were NFL football games, professional baseball games on my big screen tv!

I think I started shedding tears considering the fact that I had not seen any sports on this television in years, I looked at the screen with my mouth wide open for about ten minutes in amazement as Jon Jon went back to playing on his cell phone. He made this all possible because he simply read the manual! I guess that I am not as smart as I thought I was.

FOCUS YOUR THINKING

I think one of the most terrifying times in my life was when I first learned to drive. Driving seemed easy until the day I was put behind the wheel for the first time with my Dad teaching me. Yes, I was in driver education at school, but it seemed different when it came to my Dad teaching me, it seemed rather scary.

"Hold onto the wheel, use your eyes instead of your head when looking around, let the weight of the car fall into the curve when going through mountain like curves" he constantly advised me.

But his famous statement was, "Junior stay focused."

Out of everything he taught regarding driving, why was this particular statement the most important? Staying focused requires putting all your energy into it especially when it comes to serving God.

With everything going on in the world today, it's easy to get distracted and lose focus on what you are doing allowing something else to steal your attention. Believe me, distractions are a tactic from the enemy keeping our minds away from things that matters most.

> It's easy to get distracted and lose focus on what you are doing!

Apostle Paul gives 8 good things to keep our mind and thoughts in the right place when he says,

"Finally, brothers, whatever things are true, whatever things are honest, whatever things are just, whatever things are pure, whatever things are lovely, whatever things are of good report, if there is any virtue, and if there is any praise, think on these things"(Philippians 4:8 kjv).

The Holy Spirit dwelling within you will give you power to think and to change the way you think! What do you spend most of your day thinking about?

Are your thoughts, "True" according to what scripture says? Are your thoughts pure and honest and just or do you find your thoughts being defiled and morally unclean? With everything, keep your focus on Christ.

Begin today removing negative thinking and negative speaking from your mind and take control over what comes out of your mouth because we eat the words we speak and our words will produce what comes out of our mouth! Speak LIFE and God will give life. Speak HEALING and God will heal you. Speak PROSPERITY and God will provide all your needs.

SLOW DOWN

The prophet Habakkuk yells out, "How long oh Lord, how long?" None of us wants to wait for anything. To be totally honest about it, slowing down and waiting can be a hard things for many of us. It seems like our whole life is nothing but a rush? People rushing to get to work tailgating each other just to see who can get to the next stop light first then only to wait another ten seconds for it to turn again. Rushing to hurry home to cook, rushing to get to sleep and then rushing to get up the next morning just to start the day all over again. Is it me or do it seem like the whole world is in a rush? Maybe it is me because the whole world is on a time system that dictates where and when you need to be. Whatever the case, God wants you to slow down.

Yes, God wants you and I to slow down but is it going to hinder us or cause us to become lazy? Standing in a grocery line or waiting for the red light to change, we want everything to be done on our timing. But, God always gives solutions. Running through the airport, God gives us moving sidewalks. Waiting in long grocery lines, God gives us self-check lines where you can check out at your own pace. Life has been made living so easy for people to the point that you rarely have to leave the house for anything anymore as long as you have a cellphone.

You need groceries or anything, just make a phone call and it can be delivered to your doorstep, but the food still needs to be cooked, oh wait a minute just make another call and your food can be cooked and delivered to you as well!

Years ago, when you needed an oil change for your car you had to make an appointment which at times could well be a week or two out. Once there you had to sit in the waiting room while the oil change was being done. Now you can just drive into a dock, get your oil change and you are done in less than fifteen minutes all without you ever getting out your car like going through a drive through at a restaurant.

When my wife and I brought our first home we had to sign what seemed like over a hundred documents and the whole closing process took over two hours and even then we both felt as though we were signing away our lives and worse we felt many things were missed or overlooked in the forty-page mortgage agreement.

Now with buying our second and third home, all we had to do was tap a line and every page of the document was signed and believe or not the whole closing process took less than a half an hour and most of that time was spent talking to the lawyer. And again, I felt for sure something was missed or overlooked but everything was in order and completed correctly.

> God wants us to slow down because it is the best way hearing His voice.

God wants us to have patience and to slow down because it is the best way to hear His voice. Think about it, can you really hear what the Lord is speaking to you while you are in the midst of the midday traffic or when the baby is crying and needs immediate attention? No, He wants us to lie down and drink from the still waters (Psalms 23:2 kjv). He wants us to slow down and be still with no interruptions so that we can hear His voice clearly when He is speaking or we will miss it.

TAKE CONTROL

You might not be able to control what people say about you, you might not be able to control how people treat you but, one thing you can control is how you respond. They will push every button to find your breaking point.

People will intentionally irritate you just to learn more about your character. Many people will test you just to get a response out of you but you just have to remember to adjust your mind to respond accordingly and not in a way that will take you out of character. In all actuality, a lot of times the way we treat and see others, you will find that it is a direct reflection of how we see and treat ourselves.

No matter what you are going through, when you keep your focus on God, scripture say, "No weapon formed against you will prosper." Let's take a look at a few who found themselves in a predicament but stayed their minds focused on God:

* **Peter** *finds peace in the midst of a storm while his eyes were focused on Jesus(Matthew 14:28-29 kjv).*
* **Daniel** *was thrown in the lion's den but, he continued to believe and serve God(Daniel 6:16 kjv)*
* *Just before* **Stephen** *was stoned he gets a vision Jesus standing at the right hand of God(Acts:7:56 kjv).*

You just have to remember that as long as Jehovah Jireh and Jehovah Rapha exist in your life, He will provide and He will heal and there will always be hope. Keep your heart and mind focused on Jesus alone.

Reflection and Relevant Questions

1. Early in this chapter there was an illustrations of Minutemen and firefighters having to always be ready and on high alert. As a vessel for Christ, how are you preparing yourself to be on high alert for the coming of Christ? Do you feel it is possible to always be ready standing alone for Him?
2. If you are to be an open Vessel for Christ, how can God fill with His glory to be used by Him efficiently ?
3. With so much heartache and pain that comes with being a teenager these days, how are you as an adult preparing our future generations to deal with future issues?

PART III

THE FUNCTION
OF A VESSEL

A Vessel of Honor is one who openly exemplifies
and carries out the purposeful will of God
under the leadership of His son Jesus Christ.

14

>>»»»»» «««««««

THE POWER OF ONE

I can do all things through Christ which
strengtheneth me. (Philippians 4:13 kjv)

 hen I was younger, there was a particular Saturday
morning cartoon jingle that used to come on the
television which had a character that sang, *"One is
the loneliest number that you'll ever do, two can be
as bad as one it's the loneliness number since the number one"* in
which I knew all the words and would sing along with it at every
commercial.

But, have you ever thought just how real that one word is? "One,"
one shoe is not enough, one wheel on a bike would make it difficult
to ride, one leg would make it difficult to walk.

Having only one thing in many cases would be very hard
attempting certain task especially when you need at least two but,
what about the times when there are no other choices and you only
have one available? What about YOU being that only one?

What about times when out of an entire crowd you are the only one
that can handle a situation? What about working at a huge business
firm and you are called from home to head back to work because you
are the only one with the knowledge and experience enough to solve
a computer malfunction?

Sometimes acting alone, being alone, can at times be rather difficult and at other times it can become exceedingly rewarding.

TRYING A DIFFERENT APPROACH?

My friend has this Aunt her name was Louise. Louise was a great cook especially known around the neighborhood for her deliciously fried chicken. Louise had recently retired from a job that she had worked for many years but was now sitting at home getting more bored as each day passed by. Her nephew advised her to perhaps look for a part time job nothing too serious just something she enjoyed doing to pass the time, so she did.

Louise applied for a job and would you know it, KFC hired her. She got the job and the manager asked Louise what position she was looking for and immediately Louise replied, "Cook." Louise started frying the chicken according to the famous KFC recipe but she felt that it needed more.

After sometime, Louise began to feel that she could make the chicken taste a little better so she started adding some of her own personal delicious spices she had been using at home for years, because people loved her chicken but it completely changed the taste of the original recipe.

Just after three weeks, people began to complain about the taste, they found out what Louise was doing and she was fired. She went home and told her nephew the bad news everything that had took place the last couple of weeks and how she intended to improve the taste of the chicken.

The nephew said, "Aunt Louise, It is good to have your own ideas and recipes, but you can't go into a restaurant and try to change the menus or anything especially when certain things have been working successfully and positively for them for years."

The point I am trying emphasize to you my dear reader is that if you have been doing things a certain way and it seems to be working fine for you, stick with it even when new ideas come along, new is not always better

But, it is always good to think differently and try new and fresh ideas especially when you can apply them when and where they are needed.

Thinking differently as Louise did earlier with her added ingredients to KFC, she was simply looking at things from a different point of view or from a different approach from everyone else's, it's not about smarts or intelligence it's about thinking differently that's all. I think that they should have hired Louise back.

Now everybody has heard of the very successful computer company CBX! They have strived and have dominated the entire computer industry for years, but it has not always been that way.

For years CBX, had been getting very good results and positive feedback from a computer program they called "ETRON" which they designed and built to help not only their company but other companies computer system run more efficiently as well.

But now the time had come for a reconfiguration and a total over hall of the computer program because recently many companies had reached the point to were ETRON was becoming less useful and outdated.

Many expert programmers had come in from all around the world to help CBX come up with an updated version for ETRON, but it seemed like everything that was tried was taken off the table because it always led back to what the original ETRON was already providing.

Everyone was trying to move ETRON step by step forward until most of the programmers had given up hope and was truly believing that the days of this once popular program were over.

One night one of the programmers had went home to play with his four-year-old child Daniel and the child asked him a simple question: Daddy, "Where do babies come from?" His Dad had an answer, but he had to explain it in the simplest way he could so that Daniel would be able to understand it as a four year older would, so the Dad explained it like this:

"Well Daniel, Mommy and Daddy asked for a baby, Babies come from heaven. Jesus picks the right baby and tells a angel to take the baby to Mommy and Daddy. While Mommy and Daddy are lying in bed the angel places the baby in mommy's arms for you and I. The angel and the baby came from heaven. Sometime, God will have to explain things to us in an infant manner as if we are babies, for us to understand things in a mature way.

> Sometime, God will have to explain things to us in an infant manner as if we are babies, for us to understand things in a mature way!

The child completely satisfied with Dad's answer simply said "OK" and walked away and the Mom standing on the stairs, looking on with two slight claps of her hands just smiled. The Dad figured that he had to make the answer as simple as possible so he explained it from a backwards point of view to give an answer of understanding to his child.

The next day at work, in another meeting working on ETRON. Heads still boggled as what to do, the Dad thought about his child Daniel how he came up with a solution thinking and solving a question from a different approach. The Dad spoke up in the meeting and asked everyone "How about if we work from a backwards point of view starting from the solution and work backwards to get to where we are now to figure out where the problem lies?"

The Head CEO frowned, scratched his head a couple times, and said, "Wait a minute, he just might be on to something, we all know what the companies are looking for from ETRON, Let's try his approach."

Not soon afterwards, a solution was found, and ETRON was working more efficiently than ever before and went on for many more years thanks to one computer programmer who chose to think differently from the status quo.

> "There are many devices in a man's heart; nevertheless the counsel of the Lord, that shall stand" (Proverbs 19:21 kjv).

God has chosen you to think differently outside the box. Thinking differently begins first of all with God …and thinking of course. God has given you a mind to use especially for His glory. And don't forget, a little bit of praying goes a long way.

Through prayers, you will see things and explain things differently from everyone else.

Some may even call you "Peculiar" but it's OK because God already said:

> "But ye are a chosen generation, a royal priesthood,
> an holy nation, a peculiar people" (1 Peter 2:9 KJV).

As a Vessel of Christ, there are going to be many days when you are going to be considered peculiar or different because you thought differently or you looked at things from a different point of view from everyone else's approach but you came up with the right solution probably before they did.

A problem may occur in school, on the job or simply out for the evening with friends but, God has given you a clear mind and a beautiful heart to think for yourself. It's ok to be different. Yes there are going to be rules and guide lines to follow but, there can always be a better way of doing things or solving a problem other than what is written or the status quo. God always has a better way of doing things.

What if Henry Ford would have stopped inventing cars with the model T? We would not have the luxuries riding in cars we have today. What if God had stopped with Adam and Eve wearing fig leaves to cover themselves well, I won't go into that. Point I'm making here is that you don't have to compromise and agree with what the crowd is saying, it is ok to be yourself and to think things from a different approach, your way just might be the best and most efficient way!

DENY COMPRIMISING

Several years ago a major bank was being held up by terrorist with hundreds of workers being held hostage. The terrorist demanded ten million dollars in cash and a jet for a quick escape. The negotiators response "Sorry, but we do not negotiate with terrorist!"

I ask you my dear reader, what are you compromising in your life? Believe it or not there are people who will give up their identity just to be accepted, to be a part of the in crowd at the expense of losing a relationship with Christ. Are you giving in to ungodly ways of the world to be in a good relationship with your children or perhaps you are giving in to open lies at work in order to keep a job? Whatever the case, you are compromising.

> Therefore to him that knoweth to do good, and doeth it not, to him it is sin (James 4:17).

If you had an agreement between your child and you told them to be in the house at eleven and they came stepping in the door at eleven fifteen, either they are breaking the rules or you are going to compromise and let it slide. How will you handle this situation? The sad thing about this is that even when they continue to disobey the rules, many times they are actually rewarded by not being disciplined.

Sticking to your word or initial agreement carries weight. Giving in on an agreement you made shows that you are double minded and can easily be manipulated. People, especially children will test and challenge adults, co-workers will push you to the limits just to see how far they can take you before you snap and give in, these are times when you have to be strong. Look over the initial agreement you made and try to stick with it especially if it is beneficial.

DEVELOPING A COVENANT AGREEMENT

As an Ordained Minister, I recently had the pleasure of officiating the marriage of one of my daughters in holy matrimony to her husband. During a certain part of the ceremony they pledged their loving devotion to each other by agreeing to the marriage vows and showing and the giving of rings to each other. It was indeed a beautiful ceremony and in reality, they were not only making a covenant agreement to each other but in reality, they were signing a spiritual contract in heaven to each other.

As I read the agreement to each of them separately, they each responded by saying "Yes." The vows were made and spoken in front of witnesses but, when God became involved, it became a contract meant to last until death did them part. After that, the marriage vows and the covenant was sealed between the two of them and God.

When you make a covenant agreement with someone it requires the giving of yourself to another to fulfill a promise that was made between two parties.

When you establish a covenant relationship with Christ, it becomes one of the many blessings we have through our salvation in Christ Jesus. It becomes a bond and you are saved by grace.

God made five covenants in the Bible with men and each covenant had four distinct things in common. They each included a Promise, each had Terms, each had a Token or the shedding of blood and finally they had a Seal. The first covenant was actually made with Abraham but let's begin with Adam.

1. *Adamic covenant*: This is the covenant God made with Adam in the Garden of Eden. God promised Adam: "dominion over the earth to mankind and life everlasting in return for obedience." Genesis 3:19 kjv

   The Terms: He was not to eat from the tree of knowledge. The Token or the Shedding: He took a rib from Adam and gave one to Eve, and the Seal: The tree of life.

   God made covenants with four other men in the Bible. Each had the same four things in common. They all included a promise, they had terms, they had a token or blood was shed and they each had a seal. Here are the other four other men God made covenants with in the Bible:

2. (Noah) *Noahic covenant: read Genesis 9:11*
3. (Abraham) *Abrahamic covenant: read Genesis 12:1-3*
4. (Moses) *Mosaic covenant: Read Exodus 3:11-15*
5. (David) *Davidic covenant: Read 2 Samuel 7*

God is looking for you to be a vessel for Christ and for you to make covenant agreement with Him. He has promised to give you everlasting life, exceedingly and abundantly more than you could ever imagine. He is only asking you to serve and follow Him, that's all. A covenant with God can be as simple as: "Lord, if you remove this alcoholic drinking habit from me, I promise not to drink alcohol again the rest of my life" simple as that.

But, there are consequences involved when you go back on your own words. After you have been delivered from alcoholism and you go back and decide that one little beer can't do you no harm, you have just reneged on the contract.

You just might find that drinking habit you once had and were delivered from had come back and is now three times more worse than before you made a covenant agreement, be careful. The Bible tells us to "cease from (our) own works (Heb. 4:10 kjv), cease from 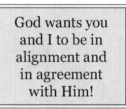 your own struggling, cease from your own plans." These are acts of faith opening up ourselves to God's presence. It would be best, if you are not sure you can keep your word to not go into agreement with someone especially with God rather than going into one and fail.

God wants you and I to be in alignment and in agreement with Him, the question is: Are you willing to make covenant with Him? The answer should be an undoubtedly, "YES."

Yes, God had covenants between He and His servants which was an agreement between the two and when they obeyed the Lord, He rewarded them. God made a covenant agreement between He and Noah. That if Noah would build an ark, He promised to never destroy the earth by flood (Gen. 9:8-15 kjv).

Yes, God made a covenant agreement with Abraham, that if he would leave his country and his father's house and go into an unfamiliar land, He would make him the father of many nations (Gen. 17:4-7 kjv) and would give him and his descendants the land of Israel-the promise land (Gen. 12:1 kjv).

God will always stand by His Word and it is necessary that you stand by yours.

Reflection and Relevant Questions

1. Describe a time when you compromised on an issue and later regretted it, because you were pressured to giving in.
2. Has there ever been a time in your life when a problem arouses and out of all the people around, you were the only one who could solve or fix the problem because you looked at the situation from a different approach? Describe how you handled it.
3. "Being in alignment with God," what does this statement mean to you?

15

>»>»>»>»>» ««««««««

ANNOINTED STRUGGLES

Who is it that overcomes the world? Only the one
who believes that Jesus is the Son of God.
(1 John 5:5 kjv)

y father was a great man who knew how to talk to
people and to his children. He could talk with friends,
coworkers, family members whoever for hours and
would always end the conversation with either a hug
or a handshake.

His talks with me were very meaningful and effective because
the advice he gave and his words have stuck with me since I was a
child. He would give an example then give his advice so that I would
understand especially the time I was debating whether on going to
college or getting a job after high school.

"The difference between a person having an education and a
person not having one" Dad told of the struggles he has had to endure
in life by not having the opportunity to get an education or to go to
school and that I needed all the education I could get.

Regarding his struggle he gave me this example and asked me
the question, "Can you tell the difference between an eagle and a
crow when they are in the air" I said, "No." Dad said, "An eagle
sores when it is in the air and a crow struggles to stay in the air." I

thought about that for a while, "Why does the crow have to struggle so hard to stay in flight when flying actually seems to be enjoyable and easy for the eagle?" Dad explained that an eagle's wings are light and strong making it easier to fly while on the other hand the crow's wings are heavy and thick and sticks to its chest while flying making it harder to fly. Dad said, "Be like an eagle and sore, get that education son."

Have ever wondered for one moment why life for some has always seemed to be a struggle and for others life seemed to come easy as if they did not have a care in the world? While many people struggle fighting everyday battles they fail to realize that while they are fighting a physical battle it is actually spiritual.

> "For we wrestle not against flesh and blood, but against principalities against powers, against the rulers of the darkness of this world, against spiritual wickedness in high places" (Ephesians 6:12 KJV).

Apostle Paul when speaking to the church at Ephesus, he explains that your struggle is not with the physical world but spiritual:

> "For we wrestle not against flesh and blood, but against principalities, against powers, against the rulers of the darkness of this world, against spiritual wickedness in high places" (Ephesians 6:12 KJV).

Pharaoh thought that he could control his kingdom by killing all the new born male babies, but while he was working in the physical, God was working in the spirit by saving just one baby, Moses, who would lead the Israelites out of Egypt, across the Red Sea into the promise land, hallelujah!

Your struggle is not with your spouse or other people but you are up against principalities, powers against rulers of the darkness and spiritual wickedness in high places. Your battle is not even of this world but you are fighting things much deeper in heavenly places and as long as you continue fighting the physical you will never win. That is why we need to have a spiritual mindset in order to fight what is really going on up in the spiritual realm.

I must say to you my dear friend that being a Vessel for Christ and living a Christian life especially for one who is carrying out the word of God to others can at times become a tussle and a struggle.

To tell you the truth, just staying faithful to reading your Word, staying faithful attending church, heck, just staying faithful to one another can become a struggle in itself, don't you agree?

God has never promised that this journey would be an easy one. He never said that all of our days would be filled with light, love, and happiness but, He did promise that He would never leave us and that we would never be alone. Actually, He says to those experiencing trials or difficulty to, "COUNT IT ALL JOY" because He has a crown for those who will endure until the end (James 1:2 kjv).

Yes, you may see folks posting pictures of them driving in the most expensive cars, yes, you may see them standing inside of a mansion but remember this, never be envious of anything or anyone else because you don't know what they had to do to get it and you for sure don't know what they are doing to keep it!

People are so worried about *post*ing things imagining who they are not and watching people *post* things of who they wish they really want to be, while in reality we all need to be focused on who we *post* to be in Christ!

Besides that, most post are just a picture. You can go to any car lot and take test drives and take pictures with as many cars as your heart's desire. You can also stand next to a nice-looking house, take a picture and people will assume that you own it. I ask you one question: Are you in love with what you imagine or are you in love with God?

You are your own person and you don't have to compare your life to anyone else's, just be yourself. Think about this, "Do the world really need two more of the people you are trying to imitate?" Maybe the world is a great and better place by

> You are your own person and you don't have to compare your life to anyone else's!

151

you, just being you! Besides, the Lord will never bless you when you are impersonating someone else.

We all go through struggles and we all have our bouts of hard times but like I emphasized earlier "You survived and you made it through!" Have you ever thought for a moment that some of the stuff that you go through is not all about you or for you, but to benefit someone else, think about that as well.

Believe me my dear reader, that there are going to be things in life that you won't be able to pass off to someone else just because you have the authority to do so, you are going to have to face up and deal with it. We all deal with never ending bills, family struggles, health issues, and yes, life is hard but we have reassurance from God that whatever struggles we may face, we can count it all joy because He will be right by our side, just don't get discouraged.

AHAB'S STRUGGLE

Ahab was one of the one's who was in a long line of evil kings who did evil in the sight of God in the history of Israel. Before the reign of Omri his father, "Ahab did more evil than any of the evil predecessors before him" (1 Kings 16:30 kjv). Starting with marrying an evil woman who had a distinct hatred for the people of God named Jezebel (1 Kings 18:4 kjv). Because of his marriage to Jezebel, a pagan woman, Ahab devoted himself to worshipping the false god Baal (1 Kings 16:31 kjv).

Ahab's second area of concern was with his confrontation with Elijah. Elijah was a prophet and a praying man of God was sent to Ahab to announce that there would be no dew or rain whatsoever, except as he commanded. him.

Ahab put the blame on Elijah for the three and a half years of famine (1 kings 18:17 kjv) because Elijah had proclaimed there would be no rain except at his command but in all actuality, it was Ahab's fault for the dry drought because he continued to follow Baalim their false god (verse 18) who he and his worshippers depended on to provide rain and good crops.

As you can see, mean ole Ahab was not about to take responsibility or the blame for the suffering of his nation. God had to demonstrate through Elijah that the Lord alone was in control of the natural world and not the false god they were serving. God prepared Elijah and again He was sent to Ahab to announce that would send rain (1 Kings 18:1-4 kjv).

To Ahab, this was not enough to prove who was the real deal, who was the true God, so Elijah issued a challenge to Ahab. He urgently called all of Israel along with 450 prophets of Baal and 400 prophets of Asherah to meet with him at Mount Carmel.

Elijah must have been pretty confident in God and powerful because of the odds, 950 to 1(1 Kings 18:19). It was time for a final faceoff between the two to prove a point, Who is the true God?

I guess at this point, the people had to make up their minds who they would believe in, The true and living God, the God of Abraham, Isaac, and Jacob or would they continue to serve and follow their false god, Baal?

These were the terms set by Elijah: On one side, the 450 prophets of Baal who would build a alter and receive a sacrificial bull. On the other side stood Elijah alone who would also build a alter and receive a sacrificial bull. Each party would then call upon their deity to set their offering ablaze. "The God who answers with fire" Elijah said, "he is God" (1 Kings 18:24 KJV).

The false prophets got to go first. After slaughtering the bull they called on their god, Baal from morning until noon. They began shouting, screaming around the alter for a response even cutting themselves so that blood gushed all over them hoping for something to happen. But even after all this, no response from Baal, complete silence.

I know it is bad to mock people especially when it is done to you or I, but Elijah began to mock the prophets and their god. He began saying to the prophets of Baal, "Maybe he is thinking it over" Elijah said. Maybe he has wandered away...Perhaps he's sleeping (1 Kings 18:27 KJV).

I guess putting the people of Israel through so much havoc with the drought and all, Ahab and Baal probably deserved to be mocked, would you agree?

Elijah wanted to make it clear that the false god and religion they were serving was the cause for God to place judgement on them. When it was finally proven that Baal did not come through for them, Elijah called the people to come to the Lords alter.

Elijah used twelve stones representing the twelve tribes of Israel to build the alter and filled it with wood. To make the odds even bigger, He called for the prophets to pour gallons of water over the alter and the sacrifice to prove that everything was wet because no man can put ablaze such a thing, only God.

Elijah prayed a prayer like nobody's business. He requested that Israel's God would be glorified and recognized as the only true and living God by the people that day. And also that Elijah was his prophet and that their hearts would be turned back to Him. My dear reader, for God to be glorified and for his people to be edified is all that God is asking for and this is the kind of prayer that will get results and answers from Him, can I get an amen?

God really did indeed answer Elijah's prayer. By the time the false prophets had finished what they were doing, it was now evening (1Kings 18:36 kjv) getting dark, the perfect time to display such a blaze. Fire fell from heaven, consuming, the wood, the stones the dust and even licking up the water (1 Kings 18:38 kjv) all of it was gone.

It was quite clear to everyone that they had just witnessed something supernatural, (something their god Baal could not do in addition to not bringing the rain.) They realized that only the true and living God could perform such

> After that, they fell down on their knees and confessed, "The Lord, He is the God!

things as providing rain and fire. After that, they fell down on their knees and confessed, "The Lord, He is the God; the Lord, he is the God"(1 Kings 18:3 kjv).

> "At the name of JESUS, every knee should bow, of
> things in heaven, and things in earth, and things under
> the earth; And that every tongue should confess that

Jesus Christ is Lord, to the glory of God the Father"
(Philippians 2:10-11 kjv).

Yes, every knee will bow down and confess that Jesus Christ
is Lord but, it is a shame the extent the Lord has to sometimes go
through to prove to us that the things in which we hold a tight grip
on to and are trying to preserve and keep, it could be money, things
or personal possessions are the very things He is trying to remove
out and from us that we may be blessed. Ahab <u>was holding onto a
false god while we are failing to realize what's actually keeping and
preserving us, but God alone!</u>

In every human being there is a yearning to worship. Either
worshipping a job or the number of followers they have on the
internet. God alone wants your worship
and you alone must make that decision.
Worship is everything and Satin wants
your worship too because he wants to exalt
himself above God. He will even go as far
as trying to put his plan into leaders of the church. People are to love
their Pastors, I love mine, but they are not to be worshipped. Look at
celebrities, where people will stare, faint and put them on a pedestal
and even bow down at the sight of just seeing them, but they are not
to be worshipped. Worshipping a person is idolatry. Satin will
struggle for the worship in your heart that's why it always remind us
in the book of Revelation:

> God alone is the only one deserving of our Worship!

> "Fear God, and give glory to Him; for the hour of
> His judgement is come: and worship Him that made
> heaven, and earth, and the sea, and the fountains of
> water." (Rev. 14:7 kjv)

God alone is the only one deserving of our Worship! We are not
just serving a god, we are serving THE GOD who loves us as His
own. In Christ we are victorious but, just as in the book of Joshua,
the people of Israel had a choice and decision to make. Joshua told

them "Choose ye this day whom you will serve." The time is now my dear reader, when you alone must also make the decision whom you will worship and serve as well, not tomorrow or next week but, *this day.* You have the victorious in Jesus Christ!

Now, here we find in chapter 18 of second Chronicles where King Ahab is ready to go into battle against the Syrian men of Samaria, What? It was just proven to him who the true God was, now he has to be taught to listen to God.

Ahab had four hundred prophets and chose Jehoshaphat to assist him in the battle against Ramothgilead (1 Kings 22:4 kjv). All four hundred deceived prophets of Ahab advised him that it was ok to go into battle and that he would come out on top but Jehoshaphat a praying man asked Ahab "if he had at least one prophet who would call upon the Lord for advice before going into battle?"

Ahab replied, "There is yet one man (Micaiah vs 8) by whom we may enquire of the Lord, but there is a little problem I have with him, I hate him; for he never prophesized good unto me, but always evil" (2 Chronicle 18:8 KJV).

The prophet Micaiah advised King Ahab that if he went into battle with Syria, he and his army would be defeated but Ahab chose rather to listen to his four hundred deceived prophets and decided to go into battle against the Syrians anyway. As you can see here that Ahab not only had a problem with his hatred of Micaiah, but he also had a problem with listening as well.

Ahab's hatred and refusal to listen to the advice of one true prophet eventually cost him his life in the battle in the end (2 Chronicles 18:34 kjv).

Why is it so hard for us realize who God is or is it that we would rather choose to listen to the crowd of false prophets as opposed to adhering to the advice of one true prophet who we really knows and has the best advice for us?

We depend on money until it runs out. We choose to listen to the negativity of a life-long friend as opposed to listening to a prayer warrior who hears from the Lord. As adults we choose to listen to gossiping friends as opposed to hearing from the Lord and end up, well I don't want to say. Where did we go wrong?

Take a lesson from King Ahab:

* Until you can develop discernment and be corrected by God, you will never be empowered by God.
* Choose God and listen to what He has to say, simple as that.

OK, now take for instance, Saul. Saul was also man who was disobedient. The Lord gave Saul one duty to perform and that was to go and destroy the Amalekites(1 Samuel 15:3). How simple is that? That meant destroying everybody and everything: man and women who were all sinners, infants and suckling, ox and sheep, camel, and ass until all was destroyed, that's it.

Now Saul did what he was commanded to do, he destroyed everything and everybody but, where Saul's mistake and disobedience came into play was when he spared the life of Agag, the king of the Amalekites. Maybe they were good friends and had a history but The Lord told Saul to destroy the Amalekites, He did not say spare certain one's, did He? I am

> To obey is better than to sacrifice.
> 1 Sam 15:22 KJV

sure that Saul had good intentions and was probably thinking that he was doing a good deed by sparing the life of a king, but by sparing the life of King Agag, it allowed his leniency and his descendants to continue the destructive, murderous ways of the Amalekites 400 years later, a major mistake.

RESULT OF AGAG'S DISOBEDIENCE

One of Agag's descendants was a man by the name of Haman who appeared on the scene 400 years later (Esther 3:1 kjv). Haman was a high-ranking political advisor under the rule of King Ahasuerus. Haman just like his forefather Agag, had it out for the Jews and his only intent was to exterminate and destroy them (Esther 3:6 kjv) especially after Mordecai's refusal to bow down to the king (Esther 3:2 kjv) which we will discuss a little later. Actually, this was only one of the terrible outcomes resulting from Agag's disobedience.

What about the time Moses approached Pharaoh pleading with him to let God's people go free to serve Him?

> Pharaoh summoned Moses and Arron and said, "Intreat the Lord, that He may take away the frogs from me and from my people; and I will let the people go, that they may do sacrifice unto the Lord." Moses said, "when shall I intreat for thee" Pharaoh said. "To morrow," Moses replied, "Be it according to thy word that thou mayest know that there is none like unto the LORD our God" (Exo. 8:8-10 kjv).

The lesson that both of these two people failed to learn is this:

First, Saul was instructed to destroy the Amalekites, but he chose to spare the life of, King Agag. If he had obeyed and done as he was instructed and destroyed them all, this would have prevented future suffering of the Jews, (Esther 3). God knows our tomorrow, years from now even generations from now! It's important to follow God's instructions specifically and not your own compassion!

And as far as mean ole Pharaoh is concerned, because of his selfish pride, he chose to allow his kingdom to suffer ten plagues upon Egypt including water turning into blood and the plague of frogs. When Pharaoh suggested to Moses to take away the frogs, "To morrow" I guess he did not take in consideration that frogs would continue to be present in his bed another night as well.

Pharaoh chose to sleep with frogs overrunning in his bed overnight rather than obey God's word by not letting the Israelites go free! Talking about a man with a huge ego, think about it, this guy chose to sleep with frogs rather than obeying God.

But let me ask you a question my dear reader. Why do you think that Pharaoh chose to have Moses remove the frogs,

> "Pride goeth before destruction, and an haughty spirit before a fall" Proverbs 16:18 (KJV).

"Tomorrow" instead of immediately? I thought about that and I came up with my own conclusion, the man simply had a lot of pride.

Pharaohs magicians could duplicate most everything that Moses did for example: turning the water into blood, rods turning into snakes and even summoning frogs, but they could not summon gnats(Exodus 8:16-19 kjv), call down hailstones(Exodus 9:22-26 kjv) nor could Pharaoh's magicians get rid of the frogs. Proving that he needed help from a more powerful god, Moses GOD! The God of Abraham, Isaac and Jacob.

The average man realizing that this was a punishment from God would have said a long time ago, "You all are free, get out of my country and take those frogs with you."

The whole country suffered because of one man's pride. Actually it took him to lose everything even sacrificing the one thing most precious to him, the life of his own child before he finally fell to his knees and surrendered to God. Remember this my dear reader,

IT IS BETTER TO OBEY THAN TO SACRIFICE!

ARE YOUR PRAYERS BEING HEARD?

Why is praying even needed? What is the importance of praying? Are there different levels of praying? First off, Praying is very important because it is one way of communicating with God. When we pray to God, we are either making a request, thanking Him, or simply talking to Him personally.

But, have you ever tried to pray and felt as though no one was listening or even felt that there was no hope in even trying to pray because the situation seemed hopeless from the start? I am here to tell you that there is hope in praying but, you still may have to cry out of desperation, "Holy, Holy Holy Lord God Almighty" in order for you to get to where you need to be.

Take for example Hannah. Hannah was the mother of Samuel. She was a woman in a crisis. She was barren and wanted a child badly. Hannah cried out to the Lord for a child until her prayers became what you would consider a prayer out of desperation.

She prayed constantly for a child until it got to the point to where she felt that her prayers were not being answered or heard. Let's take a look at Hannah's dilemma.

Hannah, the mother of Samuel had an issue. She was barren, in other words her womb was closed up and she could not have children(1 Samuel 1:6 kjv). Year after year day after day she would cry out to the Lord hoping for a miracle. But on this one particular day, this one particular prayer

> Hannah cried out to the Lord so much that her prayers became what you would call, desperate.

had to be different from the usual petitions and cries for a child. It needed to be one out of desperation, to be essential and right to the point.

> "And she vowed a vow, and said, O LORD OF HOST, if thou wilt indeed look on the affliction of thine handmaid, and remember me, and not forget thine handmaid, but wilt give unto thine handmaid a man child, then I will give him unto the Lord all the days of his life, and there shall no razor come upon his head" (1 Samuel 1:11 kjv).

She was Giving away something valuable to receive something valuable

I guess Hannah was desperate because here it seems as though she is trying to make a deal with the Lord. If You give me not only a child but a man child, I will in return give him back to You. I will give you something if you give me something(*that sounds like a deal to me*). Hannah is bold and she means business. She not only asked for a child, but she asked for a man child in particular.

"And the Lord remembered Hannah" here we see where the one who had the problem(Hannah) meets the problem solver(God). Vs 19

The Lord remembered Hannah and she gave birth to not only a son but the Lord gave her three more sons and two daughters

(1 Samuel 2:22 kjv). When you are in a crisis, sometimes you may need to cry out of desperation and God will give back to you more than what you asked for.

Hannah could have easily given up having a child thinking it must have been the will of God or looked at Peninnah who mocked her and simply said to herself, "Who cares? I don't have time for kids." But she didn't, she did not accept her barrenness, she stuck with what she wanted, a child. She prayed until her petition became a reality.

The lesson we can learn from Hannah is that we should not accept our lack of prosperity and somehow justify it as God's will for us. Praying is the key to knocking down walls and opening up doors. Praying will cause miracles to come forth.

THE WORD VS THE WORLD

Growing up, I loved watching black and white television shows like Gun Smoke and Bonanza, well I still do. One show that I liked watching in particular was, "The Beverly Hillbillies." You remember the theme of the show, it went a little like this, "There was a man named Jed, who worked real hard to keep his family fed. Then one day while shooting for some food, and up through the ground come ma bubbling crude, oil that is, black gold, Texas tea," You remember now?

Well, the Clampett family became instant millionaires when oil was struck on their land and they moved from the backwoods hills of the Ozarks to Beverly Hills California. The plot of the story is that here we find this family with hillbilly values and traditions trying to live and survive in a luxury Beverly Hills California society and culture. It shows where the two lifestyles and cultures collided and did not work and the Clampett family became the joke of the neighborhood.

We find that same mentality even going on today where folks are trying to bring the worlds culture into God's kingdom, mixing worldly values into God's plan. All you have to do is step into a local church to find choirs mixing worldly songs in with gospel songs.

You can even find people mixing worldly dances with spiritual worship right there in front of the church and it seems like no one even notices or cares. I'm telling you that the two does not mix.

The Bible says in the twelfth chapter of Romans,

"And be not conformed to this world: but be ye transformed by the renewing of your mind, that ye may prove what is that good, and acceptable, and perfect will of God" (Romans 12:2 kjv).

How in the world are you or anyone else for that matters going to have the audacity to accept this and allow worldly ideas to infiltrate into the church? True saints will stand up and speak out and say, "Wait a minute, this is not right at all!"

We have become comfortable with men dating men, women dating women. And transgender has become such a norm in our society that you can't even look at a person anymore and know which gender they are. Let me tell you something, just because these things are accepted and are ok with the culture does not mean that it is ok with the kingdom! God is not pleased.

> You cannot mix worldly desires with kingdom purposes, the two simply do not mix together.

You cannot mix worldly desires with kingdom purposes, the two simply do not mix together. We as a culture and a society have to make a choice, either we are going to stand for Christ or not. There is no sitting on the wall anymore where you think that you have plenty time to decide. You have to make a choice.

Put it like this: If you have not made up your mind that you are completely ready to stand for Christ or you feel that you are not quite sure just yet, you can stop right there, you are a doubting Thomas, and YOU have already made up your mind!

There can be no doubt in serving Christ! Do you think that you can just sit on the wall tapping your fingers wondering if you are ready to be a soldier in the army of the LORD? You better jump down off that wall and get on the Lord's side while you can.

Sitting on the wall is a very dangerous place to be! Can you imagine yourself being in the midst of a bloody war, uniform on with your gun in hand and the enemy is coming directly at you armed and to ready to destroy you, and you are standing there tapping your fingers on the temple of your head wondering what you should do? I will leave it at that.

<u>Reflection and Relevant Questions</u>

1. In this chapter Paul talked about a woman in crisis, Hannah. She wanted something so bad that she was willing to give up something in order to receive something. What will you be willing to give up in order for you to receive what God has for you? A car, your children, worldly possessions, your life? Explain.

2. James chapter 1:2 says, "Count it all joy, when you fall into divers temptations." How can you really count something as being joyous while being tempted or going through the worst times of your life? Explain a time in your life when you felt joy during a time of bereavement and sorrow, financial issues or job loss etc.

3. In this chapter we mentioned the verse: "Be not conformed to this world: but be ye transformed by the renewing of your mind, that ye may be proved what is that good, and acceptable, and perfect will of God (Romans 12:2 kjv). What does it mean to you to be not conformed to this world? Explain

---

16

>>>>>>>> <<<<<<<<<

UTILIZING WHAT YOU HAVE

As every man hath received the gift, even so
minister the same one to another as good stewards
of the manifold grace of God (1 Peter 4:10 kjv).

omething I learned from one of my talented college professors is: **P**roper **P**re-**P**lanning **P**revents **P**oor **P**erformance (The six P's). The whole class was taught this lesson when we were told at the beginning of the school year that a major exam consisting of what we have been over could be given at any time throughout the school year.

This professor was known for doing unusual things to keep his students on their toes like giving out a pop quiz in the middle of class, taking unannounced outdoor trips to shadow with other professionals, or one time he even brought lunch for the entire class and we all sat around in a circle eating french fries discussing our future plans and goals, now remember, this is college.

So, towards the end of the school year, a shock to everyone, here comes the professor handing out this expected five-page exam. What was unexpected was that the exam only covered items we had went over the first month of the school year.

Like I mentioned earlier, he was known for doing unusual things like that to keep the class on their toes. Did I also mention that during that first month, he emphasized on several occasions the importance of reading over entire documents before working on them, whether it be an application for a job or filling out countless pages for a mortgage to read over it before signing your signature on the dotted line.

Well anyway, when it came time for our final exam, the Professor put that particular lesson to work. Now, here we are taking the final exam for the year which was going to be a third of entire year's final grade. He handed out this long ten-page exam but, there was the catch, on the very last page in a corner he had typed in small print:

> Note: "You are not required to complete this exam but, as soon as you read this note, sign it and take the exam to the front and hand it to me and leave. Your grade will be based on how much time it takes for you to turn it in, do not share this note with anyone else."
> Signed Professor Johnson

Believe it or not, it took some students less than a minute to turn in their exam papers while others were still working carefully through each and every question forty-five minutes later. I did get a "B" out of his class.

> Why do you think that it is important to plan ahead especially if God has already written out a life's plan for us?

During those school years, we all thought that this particular professor was off his rockers but to tell you the truth, he was teaching us how to think and how to use our heads. As I grew into maturity, I found his ways of teaching to become very helpful in my daily life.

But, getting back to the topic at hand, why do you think that it is important to plan ahead especially if God has already written out our life's plan for us? Why is there a need to have a strategic plan when facing issues or going into difficult battles when the Lord is on our side?

Yes, God has a plan for our lives (Jeremiah 29:11 kjv) but at the same time we are given the authority and the opportunity to make decisions and choices in our lives. I guess you can thank ole Adam and Eve for that one. Before they ate the apple from the forbitten tree in the garden, God had their whole life all laid out for them.

Their whole life was planned out and they did not have
to worry about anything, but after biting the apple (*heck,*
they did not even get to enjoy eating the whole apple)
their eyes were open and the covering that God once had
over them was now gone. Now, because of that one act,
we are responsible for the choices we make in our lives.

WHAT'S IN YOUR VESSEL?

The prophet Elisha had just solved a problem concerning three Kings (the Kings of Israel, Judah, and Edom, 2 Kings 3:13 kjv) who were at the mercy of the King of Moab. Soon after that he was about to perform a miracle for a woman who actually had money but the bills over exceeded what she had and there arose a problem, the creditor was standing at her door ready to collect:

"Now, there cried a certain woman of the wives of the sons of the prophets unto Elisha, saying, Thy servant my husband is dead; and thou knowest that thy servant did fear the lord: and the creditor is come to take unto him my two sons to be bondmen.

And Elisha said unto her, "What shall I do for thee? Tell me, what hast thou in the house?" And she said, "Thine handmaid hath not anything in the house, save a pot of oil."

Then he said:

"Go borrow thee vessels abroad of all thy neighbors, even empty vessels; borrow not a few.

And when thy art come in, thou shalt shut the door upon thee and upon thy sons, and shalt pour out into all those vessels, and thou shalt set aside that which is full.

So she went from him, and shut the door upon her and upon her sons, who brought the vessels to her; and she poured out.

And it came to pass, when the vessels were full, that she said unto her son, bring me yet a vessel. And he said unto her, There is not a vessel more. And the oil stayed" (2 Kings4:1-6 KJV).

When I think about it, besides the parting of the Red Sea, this particular passage is perhaps one of the greatest miracles mentioned in the Old Testament. The theme of this particular verse I believe is simply this: "The woman was dependent upon having an available vessel to be used." Really, How could the oil be used if there was no available vessel to put the oil in to pay the debts?

All so often we hear of people searching for a miracle but, think about this, The miracle was not so much as in the oil itself, the overall spiritual thought I got out of this that, "God is looking for available vessels among you and I to put His blessings and His overall purpose into it? It is all about the vessel, not the woman or the oil, but the vessel.

> God is saying to you, "Give me a vessel (Your heart) so I can fill it"

The verse also says, "And the creditor is come to take unto him my two sons to be bondmen" (2 Kings 4:1 KJV) meaning that if the debts were not paid, the bondage and the debt would be passed down to the next generation. In other words, the children would be enslaved.

I am telling you that the creditor and enemies are standing at the doorstep and are coming inside our homes at the present time searching out our unprotected loved ones, our children and their children's children and if we don't have a covering or protection over them they don't have a fighting chance of survival, the enemy is coming and will take them away.

Look around your home, what do you have in your home? Things will either bring a blessing a hinderance or a spiritual covering over it? What spiritual covering do you have over your home? What spiritual covering do you have over yourself? Many people believe that they should be accountable not only to God, but to a spiritual leader as well. A spiritual leader who constantly serves as an intercessory prayer warrior who covers you, your family and your household spiritually and emotionally.

But then again, people are refusing any type of covering even one over their own children. Hearts have grown cold for one reason or another either they have been hurt by the church, or simply lost faith in God. Whatever the case maybe, God is calling you! In the midst of your trials and discouragement, God is calling you. In the midst of your pain and heartbreak, God is calling you.

God is calling and saying to you, "Give me a Vessel (Your heart) so I can fill it but, we are holding back and responding by saying, "I can give you two thirds of my heart, I go to church occasionally" and God will give you two thirds of the blessings you deserve and the good things He has instore for you.

There are so many blessings that are dormant because you have not aligned yourself with God to receive them. The great thing about this is that you don't have to work for blessings but, instead you respond to what God will do for you, a blessing is a gift.

Everyone wants to know, "Lord, what is your Will for my life?" If you simply say, "Lord, I am an empty vessel, please come fill me with everything You have for me, I submit to Your Will" and The Lord will pour out a blessing that will not only overflow into your life, but will flow also into your children's life and into your home as well!

We all need a miracle in our household to protect our children today or our seed is going to be held in bondage. We need a house full of praying warriors, we need the spirit of the Holy Ghost constantly dwelling among us or else there will be no hope for our future generations to come. There is a spirit out there just waiting to enslave our next generation either by, unlawful drugs, alcoholism, addiction, etc.

> God is looking for Vessels He can use for His glory.

God is looking for vessels (You and I) He can use for His glory. One who is willing to carry out His purpose, one who is filled with the Holy Ghost and is ready to provide a covering to save the next generation from heartache and suffering that come along in this trying world today.

UTILIZING WHAT YOU HAVE

Have you ever thought that the things that you are searching for and in desperate need of could be sitting right in front of you and you not realizing it? You may have a screw driver with a flat head screw bit but are in desperate need of a Phillips screw bit *one you have spent hours ripping up the garage looking for* just to tighten one bolt.

But, what you failed to realize is that what you were in need of was right in front of you because if you pulled out the flat head bit from the driver, on the other side of that flat head screw bit was what you needed, a Phillips screw bit.

Don't you know that you can be dying of heat exhaustion sitting in a new car because you fail to utilize the AC? The same thing. You could be dying of thirst sitting in the middle of a river?

Many years ago, there was a huge vessel that was sailing at the mouth of the Atlantic Ocean where it meets the Amazon River. The huge vessel was running out of the fresh water that was stored onboard and many of the passengers began to panic and started to complain of thirst and actually, some of them had begun to start thinking they were going out of their minds dying from dehydration.

Eventually, they saw a small boat travelling nearby and they all yelled and cried out, "Can you please help us, we are dying of thirst over here, can you please spare us just a little water?"

> We have what we need right in front of us but we are either not utilizing it or failing to realize we already have it.

The man said "Sure" he reached over the side of his boat and dipped a pitcher in the water, gave it to them and said, "Here, and there is plenty more where that came from."

The people on board the huge ship did not realize that they had sailed out of the salty waters of the Atlantic Ocean into the fresh waters of the Amazon river. Many of us are like that today, we have our needs and wants right in front of us but we are either not utilizing it or failing to realize we already have it.

And at the same time you may have what you need and taking for granted the use for it. You may be complaining that you are in deep debt but look at the bright side, you still have a job. God will always supply your needs.

Moses looked for someone to speak for him to overcome Pharaoh. God supplied him with a staff which he held up and the Red Sea opened. David needed something facing Goliath when he only had a sling shot. God supplied a creek which had stones in it. God will supply all your needs so utilize what you already have.

Has anyone ever said to you, "You have a gift of singing" or "You have the gift of healing" and you looked at them with a puzzled expression. Someone may have even said to you, "Your talent is in _____" (you fill in the blank). No matter what word fills the blank, The questions are, "Have you recognized your gift or talent and are you utilizing it?"

Believe it or not many people don't utilize their gifting because they don't value it. When you value your spiritual gifting you treat it differently based on how much it really means to you. You can place a thousand one-dollar bills in front of a one-year-old child and they will probably rip the bills into pieces but replace those bills with a teddy bear and they will hug, cuddle and love on it all day because, that is what they value most especially at that age.

Same goes for grownups, the choice between the teddy bear and a thousand dollars and the grownup will snatch the money and not even look back at the teddy bear, not once. It is based on where you place your value or what values you the most.

Let's talk about gifts for a moment. I'm referring to the gifts given by God, Spiritual Gifts:

1. The Gift of Prophecy
2. The gift of Speaking in tongues
3. The gift of Knowledge
4. The gift of Wisdom

5. The gift of Discernment
6. The gift of Miracles
7. The gift of Healing

God has given each one of us a certain gift. Whether you want to utilize it or not is totally up to you, but you do have a God given spiritual gift (1 Corinthians 12:1-10 kjv).

Thirty-five years ago, I was baptized and filled with the Holy Ghost with evidence of speaking in tongues. Coming up out of the baptism pool was an experience unlike anything else I have ever experienced in my entire life. The water in the pool was extremely refreshing, my mind was clear, and I felt like an all-new person, that's the only way I can describe my experience getting baptized.

After being baptized, I soon began speaking in unknown tongues. Many folks fail to immediately realize or understand their God given gift so many times God will have to place you in certain situations for you to realize it.

Did I mention that I once suffered from being in a coma for seven days. After almost dying and eventually coming out of the coma, it took me a while getting readjusted and basically get back to a somewhat normal life.

I had to relearn walking, reading/writing, driving and even basic counting. But there was something else going on during that particular time of my life where now I can look back and see how God was working things out and preparing me for bigger and better things in my life as well. My memory was restored better than ever before. I could remember things that happened in my life when I was only three or four old, I could remember past events that others had completely forgotten

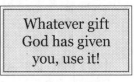

Whatever gift God has given you, use it!

about but the one thing that never left my memory, was the ability to speak to God through intercessory and speaking in tongues! Through everything that I had previously lost, ability to read, ability to write or the ability to drive, the one thing that I did not lose and remained in my soul was the gifting of the Holy Ghost and the ability to speak through intercessory pray, Halleluiah!

Sometimes, God will even give two gifts to believers. I try as much as possible and as often as possible to utilize my God given giftings, The gift of speaking in tongues, the gift of prayer and the gift of healing and encouraging.

Like I mentioned before, everyone has a God given gift. Could be cooking, could be singing, could be healing, could be listening, or even speaking. Don't let the devil put fear in you in your using of the spiritual gifting God has given you, use it to the fullest!

Reflection and Relevant Questions

1. In this chapter we talked about Spiritual Gifts. What spiritual gift/gifts did God give to you? Explain
   a. In what ways have your Spiritual Gifts benefited you, benefited others?
   b. Read (1 Corinthians 12:20) *concerning all the spiritual gifts.* "But now are they many members, yet but one body." What does this verse mean to you? Explain.

2. Who was that one person in your life who inspired you, encouraged you to utilize your gifts and more importantly led you to Christ?
3. Paul also talks about a Spiritual Covering. What spiritual covering do you have over your life either through a minister or someone praying for you through intercessory prayer?

17

>>>>>> <<<<<<<

EQUIPPTED TO LEAD

"Make you perfect in every good work to do His
will, working in you that which is well-pleasing in
His sight, through Jesus Christ; to whom be glory
forever and ever; Amen"(Hebrews 13:21 kjv)

 love watching movies. One of my all-time favorite
is, "The Titanic." I still can't believe that I teared up
when Jack froze, died and sank to the bottom of the
ocean in the movie. The Titanic equipped with the
latest technology was built in 1909 hit an iceberg and sank in 1912.
The ship was constructed of thousands of one-inch-thick steel plates
and two million steel and wrought iron rivets and sixteen watertight
compartments basically designed to be "The Unsinkable."

I always wondered how a ship of that magnitude could be built
but mostly how the disaster of its sinking could possibly have been
prevented where over 1600 people either drowned or died from
hypothermia. The problem was not the iceberg. The problem was
that the Titanic was not properly equipped.

One of the major problems was that there were not enough lifeboats
to accommodate the 1600 passengers. They were promised a luxurious
trip across the Atlantic Ocean but they did not make it because they
were not properly prepared and the Titanic was not properly equipped.

Many of us even today are just like the passengers on the Titanic and the ship itself because we are not prepared and properly equipped for battle, ready to face the trials and dangers and hardships that come with life.

1600 passengers on the Titanic did not reach their destination, but God wants you to reach your destination. Are you prepared and equipped? Let's see.

EQUIP YOURSELF

During Biblical times, the men prepared themselves properly before a fight. They would sharpen their spears to the sharpest point. They would train their horses to follow specific commands and the chariots were made of the finest wood. Men would usually fight face to face using knives and shields.

The Bible says that we should always be Biblically prepared. That we should put on the whole amour of God:

> "Put on the whole armour of God, that ye may be
> able to stand against the wiles of the devil. For we
> wrestle not against the flesh and blood, but against
> principalities, against powers, against the rulers of the
> darkness of this world, against spiritual wickedness
> in high places (Eph. 6:11-12 kjv).

We find in the book of Joshua where the Israelites were fighting a battle in the course of conquering Canaan. The Lord told Joshua according to (Joshua 6:1-27 kjv) that if the Israelites would march around the walls of Jericho once a day for six days and seven times on the seventh day blow their trumpets, the walls of Jericho would collapse, allowing the Israeli army to take the city. They were equipping themselves for battle according to God's way.

> **We should always
> be Biblically
> prepared!**

Battles today are not fought with spears or trained horses and many wars are prepared sometimes years in advance. Countries today make use of the highest of technology available rarely even seeing the opponents face. The use of satellites, submarines, fighter planes which can deliver or drop a bomb on the enemy with a precise target in mind.

We as Christians are fighting and are up against a different type of battle. Not one fighting with spears, guns or even the use of modern satellites. Our battle is not even physical but our battle is spiritual against the enemy known as Satin.

> The Lord has got you covered!

You will know when you are up against a spiritual battle because The Lord will give you a least likely object to fight with. The giant Goliath was armored with a bronze helmet, a coat of bronze mail, greaves of brass upon his legs and on his shoulders a target of brass prepared to step on David. The Lord gave David a sling shot and Goliath the giant was defeated.

The Lord gave Moses a staff when he and the Israelites were being pursued by Pharaoh and his army. Pharaoh and his army consisted of four thousand infantry men, but was defeated by Moses who only had a staff, Pharaoh had six hundred chosen captains and chariots but was defeated by Moses who only had a staff. Remember that with God all things are possible.

We prepare ourselves not with heavy armor to guard our bodies and spears to attack but with one and only amour of protection the shield of protection-The Holy Bible! Ultimately, the Lord is described as our shield of protection. No matter who or what rises up against us, The Lord has got us covered,

> The 91st book of Psalms tells us: He that dwelleth in the secret place of the most High shall abide under the shadow of the Almighty. He is my refuge and my fortress: my God; in him will I trust (Psalms 91:1-2 KJV).

God will fight battles for us if we allow Him to do so. All too often we try to overcome obstacles in our lives busting out our brains trying to figure out a game plan of attack. How are the bills going to be paid this month?

How do we train up our children and enjoy life? The answers are right there with God and in the Bible? It says to:

* Train up a child in the way he should go: and when he is old, he will not depart from it (Proverbs 22:6 KJV).
* But my God shall supply all your needs according to His riche in glory by Christ Jesus (Philippians 4:19 KJV).

And lest not forget the Oil of Joy. The Oil of Joy will put the enemy in its place giving you the opportunity to experience pure joy allowing God to do a work in your life. God wants you to have peace and enjoy life but how can you experience peace if you have no joy?

Through reading the Bible we can find that we can not only put our trust and faith in Him but that He will deliver us from the snare of the fowler and the noisome pestilence of the enemy. God also gives the angels charge over us as another shield of protection to keep us in all of our ways (Psalms 91:11-16 kjv).

So, again, I will ask you? "What do you need when facing daily trials or a spiritual battle" perhaps a few more friends or perhaps you may need a weapon?

No, you need to gird yourself up with the breastplate of righteousness, put on your helmet of salvation, shod your feet, and hold onto the shield of faith and tell the enemy to come on with it, I am ready for whatever you got, bring it on!

"What else do you need going into battle besides the Lord?" He is yours and mine and our only means protection, because that's the kind of God we serve!

He will fight your battles because He is our shield of protection. When they cried out for help against a very large multitude of enemies, Jehoshaphat, (who we know was a praying man sought the Lord when he asked king Ahab, "Is there not here a prophet of the

Lord that we might enquire of him" (2Chron 18:6) the king of Judah sought the Lord and proclaimed a fast throughout all of Judah and all

the inhabitants of Jerusalem which consisted only of their little children and their wives were told (Be not afraid nor dismayed by reason of this great multitude; for the battle is not yours, but God's (2 Chronicles 20:15 kjv). Equip yourself in the Lord.

> It's not the size of the dog in the fight, it's the size of the fight in the dog!

Be not afraid my dear reader, God has got your back and will fight the battle for you no matter the size or depth of it. Remember that old saying, "It's not the size of the dog in the fight, it's the size of the fight in the dog?"

The devil does not want your car, the devil does not even want your bank account, he wants the fight that is within you to fail! When the enemy comes up against you, fight back with the Word of God "Satin, you get thee behind me" (Matt 16:22 kjv). Whenever the enemy comes and put thoughts of suicide or self-destruction upon you, fight back with the Word of God "I shall not die but live" (Psalms 118:17 KJV) because the Lord says "He comes to give life, and to give it more abundantly" (John 10:10 kjv).

Like I mentioned a little earlier and I feel the importance of mentioning it twice because so many parents are either getting tired or have been discouraged by others and even having doubts regarding the way in which you are raising children. Remember to simply refer back to the Word of God which will remind you to "Train up a child in the way he should go: and when he is old, he will not depart from it" (Proverbs 22:6 KJV). Everything you need to know is right there in the manual, The Holy Bible. The Holy Bible was written to inform us.

THE EQUIPPED WOMEN!

Marital laws in the Bible favored men, period. Women lived under strict laws especially when it came to sexual behavior with adultery where offense was punishable by stoning. Laws regarding inheritance also favored the men. But there were many women who have played important roles in society even during Biblical times.

Some were mentioned because of their relationship with their husband and many others were mentioned because of the important role or situation they were actually involved in.

Take for example: Zipporah the wife the <u>wife of Moses,</u> now here was a woman with an attitude but, she feared the Lord enough to obey

> We may even have to stand alone especially when it comes to you obeying God!

Him even when her husband Moses apparently failed to take seriously God's commands which teaches us that sometimes we may even have to stand alone especially when it comes to you obeying God.

* Take for example: <u>Lot's wife.</u> Remember she was the one who looked back at the city of Sodom while it was being destroyed and immediately, she was turned into a pillar of salt. Here again the woman's name was not even mentioned but her involvement played made such a huge impact teaching us all an important lesson in that when God has something positive instore for you, to move forward and not to turn or look back at what the good Lord delivered or brought you out of.

* What about the <u>woman with the alabaster box</u> of oil who anointed Jesus feet with the oil. <u>The alabaster box</u> of oil was all she had to her name showing that there was no limit on what she was willing to give to Jesus. Teaching that when you give your all to the Lord, He will in turn give His all to you.

The point that I am trying to make here is that women have influenced the lives of women as well as men in the Bible from time immemorial and many of their names were not even mentioned. But, we are going to look at it a little bit deeper. In this chapter we are not only going to talk about women empowered but more importantly women of valor and those anointed by God.

Let's take a look at just a few women who were chosen and equipped by God, empowered by God to use not so much as their name but their God given position to overcome difficult situations. Take for example, Deborah.

~DEBORAH

She was a prophetess and a mighty warrior of Israel and was chosen by God to serve His people during a very difficult and challenging time. She was the fourth judge of Israel and the only female judge mentioned in the entire Bible. Let's take an insight look as to how these qualities of her came to play and saved a nation.

During a time when the people of Israel were walking away from God, a period of over twenty years of being harshly oppressed, under the wicked leadership of the King of Canaan whose name was, Jabin, the Israelites suffered greatly.

> But God was on the Israel's side which makes the difference!

The Israelites had suffered enough and finally cried out for help (Judges 4:1-3) and needed a hero to deliver them out from under the hands of King Jabin. God spoke through Deborah to lead the Israelites into battle against the mighty warriors of King Jabin.

Now, Deborah was a true woman of authority. Women of true authority know how to delegate authority. Deborah called upon a man named Barak to lead the Israelites against Jabin's mighty army. The whole Israeli nation was living in constant fear but, Barak accepted the challenge to go into battle under one condition, Deborah had to go with him. Deborah agreed and prophesied that Israel would win the battle against Jabin and Sisera, but a woman would get the credit(Judges 4:8-9 kjv).

The battle was completely lopsided because we find that Jabin's army had a multitude of fighters with over "900 chariots of iron," the height of military technology at the time, while Deborah and Barak's army consisted of only 10,000 Israelite men and women but, God was on Israel's side which makes the big difference.

After the battle not a single man of King Jabin's army survived teaching us again that when God is with you, who can be against you.

The lesson we can learn from Deborah is that when she stepped into her role as a leader even during difficult times, she showed her belief in God and found strength and empowerment in God to overcome even when the odds were against her. It also showed humbleness, in her because even though she was a high-ranking judge she called upon a man to lead her army to victory in the battle against King Jabin.

We too can be used just like Deborah was. You don't have to have a title like a judge, just believe in God that He will give you strength to endure and that He will bring you through.

Yes, bills are overdue, but believe in God that He will come through!

Yes, health issues arising, but believe in God that He will strengthen you up!

Yes, you are feeling like you are losing your mind, but believe in God that He will give you peace!

Stop looking at the odds, just remain humble and keep your focus on Him above, and as always, He will bring you through! There is something that happens when you humble yourself, supernatural things happen.

Now, what about Esther? Here was a woman who was dealing with a man (Haman)who had a generational curse on him but little did she know that God was putting her in the position and aligning her up to prevent and save an entire race from being exterminated.

~ESTHER

Many people feel that the book of Esther probably should not even be in the Bible mainly because the name of God is never mentioned in it. Besides that, Esther is only one of two books named after a woman, the other being Ruth.

> Stop looking at the odds, just remain humble and keep your focus on Him above, and as always, He will bring you through!

But God's presence is clear and alive through the experiences and actions of Esther which you will see here and I will get right to the point.

The story of Esther actually began about 400 years earlier and starts out like this. Saul was ordered to destroy the Amalekites

(1 Samuel 15:9 kjv). Saul destroyed the Amalekites because of their murderous mindset and hatred of the Jews(Israel as they came up out of Egypt, but out of disobedience, Saul spared the King of the Amalekites(Agag) allowing the family lineage of the Amalekites to continue.

The bad thing about this one act of disobedience is that the same murderous destructive spirit that was in the Amalekites against the Jews back in the book of Exodus arouse again over 400 years later in the book of Esther in mindset and heart of a wicked guy named Haman. Many of us can relate to the decision Saul made when he spared Agag. Situations that occurred many years ago that we failed to deal with at that time are now facing us years later head on with dire consequences. Now, Haman could be identified with groups such as the Romans, Nazis, Stalinists and even Hitler, people with a long history of hatred toward Jews.

Now, after Esther was born, her parents died and she was adopted by her cousin, Mordecai. Mordecai a Jew was a man who feared God so you can already see how she was being raised especially living under the rule of King Ahasuerus.

On a certain day, King Ahasuerus made a feast in the midst of the nobles of countries, and high princes showing off all his riches of his glorious kingdom, and he called for his wife Vashti, to show off her beauty in front of the guest but, she refused (Esther 1:11 kjv).

You would think that it would be rather embarrassing especially to a king when he calls for his beautiful wife and she does not show up. I guess that she had plans of her own or she simply did not want to be humiliated but, anyway she did what she did and turned down the King's invite.

Because of Queen Vashti's refusal (there became a position available for a new queen), the king made a decree (an official order) set out looking for a replacement for Vashti to be the queen:

> "Then said the King's servants that ministered to him,
> "Let there be fair virgins sought for the king: And let the
> king appoint officers in all provinces of his kingdom,

that they may gather together all the fair young virgins
unto Shushan the palace, to the house of the women,
unto the custody of Hege the king's chamberlain, keeper
of the women; and let their things for purification be
given them: And let the maiden which pleaseth the king
be queen instead of Vashti" (Esther 2:1-4 KJV).

When Esther was brought before the king, it please him more
than any of the other women that was brought before him and he
made Esther the new queen instead of Vashti (Esther 2:17 kjv).

One day Mordecai her Uncle overheard two of the kings
chamberlains plotting to overtake the kings kingdom and he told
Esther who in turn advised the king giving Mordecai the credit
(Esther 2:21-22 KJV).

At that time, wicked Haman had been promoted to be higher than
all the other princes that were with him and they bowed down to him,
all but Mordecai who had told them that he was a Jew (Esther 3:2 KJV).

After that, Haman was given authority to destroy the Jews and
he not only wanted to take out and kill Mordcai but, he also wanted to
kill all the Jews because there was a multitude of the Jewish people
in the kingdom (Esther 3:6 kjv). Hamon made a gallow especially for
Mordecai to be hung.

> When Esther was brought before the king, it please him more than any of the other women that was brought before him and he made Esther the new queen instead of Vashti

There was a night when the king could not sleep and he commanded the
book of records of the chronicles to be read to him. It was read that
Mordecai had warned of Bigthana and Tereshs plot to kill king Ahasuerus
but nothing was done to honor Mordecai for his faithful service.

The king intended to fix this oversight but needed someone to
carry out his plan to honor Mordecai but who was available?

Haman on his way to the king to get permission to kill Mordecai
entered the outer court and before he had a chance to ask for
permission to kill Mordecai, the king asked Haman, "What should

be done for the man the king wants to honor?" Haman certainly thought that the king was intending to honor him so he suggested:

"For the man whom the king delighteth to honor, let the royal apparel be brought which the king useth to wear, and the horse that the king rideth upon, and the crown royal which is set upon his head: And let this apparel and horse be delivered to the hand of one of the king's most noble princes, that they may array the man withal whom the king delighteth to honour, and bring him on horseback through the streets of the city, and proclaim before him, thus shall it be done to the man whom the king delighteth to honour"(Esther 6:7-9 KJV).

MORDECAI HONOURED

King Ahasuerus thinking this was the perfect idea to honor Mordecai hurried to do just as Haman had proposed. This humiliated Haman and his downfall began. This shows us that "with God all things are possible"(Matthew 19:26 kjv). Everything good Haman had planned and intended for himself was done to honor Mordecai the one whom he sought to kill. Imagine Haman driving around the streets shouting, "Thus shall it be done unto the man whom the king delighteth to honour' (Esther 6:11 kjv).

On the second day in a row, Esther held a feast for the king and Haman. The king asked Esther to make her request, and the king granted her anything she wanted up to half his kingdom. Esther answered: "For we are sold, I and my people to be destroyed, and to perish. But if we had been sold for bondmen and bondwomen, I had held my tongue, although the enemy could not countervail the kings damage" (Esther 7:4 KJV).

Then the king Ahasuerus said to Queen Esther, "Who is he, and where is he, that durst presume in his heart to do so?" (vs5) and Esther said, "The adversary and the enemy is this wicked Haman."

After that, the king ordered Haman to be hung. When I think about this scenario, Haman was not only being hung because he sought to kill the king and of his hatred of the Jews but in

> What the enemy has meant for evil, The Lord will intend it for your good!

185

retrospect he was being hung on same 50-cubit-high gallows which he had previously prepared for Mordecai to be hung on (Esther 7:1-10 kjv). Not only that, the letters in which Haman had originally sent out to destroy all the Jews were reversed (Esther 8:5 kjv).

What the enemy had meant for evil, God intended it for Mordecai's good, Hallelujah!

Just look at how God can work things out and make a complete turnaround just when you think life is at its worst and He can do the same for you too. God can make even your worst enemies to honor you!

After that, a decree was issued out from king Ahasuerus to every province saying:

> "Wherein the king granted to the Jews, which were in every city to gather themselves together, and to stand for their life, to destroy, to slay, and to cause to perish, all the power of the people and province that would assault them, both little ones and women, and to take the spoil of them for a prey, upon on day in all the provinces of king Ahasuerus, namely, upon the thirteenth day of the twelfth month, which is the month Adar" (Esther 8:10-12 KJV).

Basically, what this decree was saying is that the entire Jewish nation had been shown mercy and actually survived a modern-day holocaust, thanks to Esther and Mordecai! Let all the nation sing and praise Him, Blessed is the God of Israel!

WHAT THE DEVIL MEANT FOR EVIL, THE LORD MEANT IT FOR GOOD!

You may have been waiting for what seems like an eternity for a baby like Hannah, but God has meant it for good! Your health may be failing you in the instance of Job, but God meant it for Good! You don't need luck, You just need to love and keep your focus on God!

The lessons we can learn from Esther:

1. *God can use ordinary people to do astounding things.* Because of their disobedience to God, Israel was in captivity and that was the in which Esther lived. She was a Jew considered a minority race and besides her beauty, you probably could have considered her no different from anyone else. If you submit to God's will, He can use you as well.
2. *God places mentors in our lives to teach us wisdom and guidance.* Esther's uncle Mordecai not only provided parental guidance but he was also her spiritual advisor. He gave her great advice (don't share that you are a Jew)when she went into the palace with the other virgins. Mordecai was dependable and reliable because when a plot was uncovered to murder the king and all Jews he advised Esther to warn the king. This advice from her trusted advisor saved a nation.

There is no need to ask how old you may be, it does not matter at this point, Pastors and leaders, we all need God fearing, God loving mentors in our lives. One of the greatest stresses in life is not knowing what is right or wrong. That's why we need mentors who will show guidance and provide wisdom to help us get to the next level. No one wants to remain physically, mentally nor spiritually the same way as they were ten even five years ago, we all have a desire to grow. Seek advice from a mentor. Advice does not always have to come from someone who is getting paid for their time. Speak with ones whom you truly trust.

COMMISSIONED

The definition of the word "commission" is, "A formal written warrant granting the power to perform various acts or duties." Several years ago, while living in Ohio my wife and I attended a church located in a

You are now entering the mission field!

neighboring community where I was allowed to share my testimony. Upon leaving and exiting the church's parking lot there was a sign that read:

"You are now entering the Mission Field."

We both pondered over the wording because we had never seen a sign that read those words before. Leaving the parking lot I myself thought the sign was referring to someone else who was perhaps leaving the country going on a mission trip. But, that's not what it meant at all, it was referring to you and I.

When you think about it, we are always on the mission field. At work, you are on the mission field. At the store, you are on the mission field. At church, on the playground sitting with other parents, even eating dinner at a restaurant, you are always out in the mission field.

Point being here my dear reader is that it is our job to go out into the neighborhoods, hitting the streets and out into the world sharing the good news and the Word of God to everyone. Believe it or not, a simple "GOD BLESS YOU" or a simple "WAVE" to someone could possibly save someone's life or better yet lead them to Christ.

Some time ago there was a man and a woman heading to this huge conference in Alabama where they were to speak on the subject of Spiritual Healing. Driving down this ten-mile dirt road where they had not seen anyone or anything since starting to get to their destination, they drove past this old broken-down wooden house where an elderly lady was sitting alone on the front porch with her head down.

As they were driving past the house the lady in the car waved to the lady on the porch and she lifted up her head and waved back.

A day later during the conference it had come time for various ones to come to the front and give a short testimony. A lady slowly walked up to front to the podium and began to speak:

> "Several years ago my husband died, I have no children nor family. I live alone with no one to call, to talk to not to mention rarely seeing another person. A few days ago, I was contemplating suicide. As I sat on my

front porch I was near doing it with a knife in my hand. All of a sudden this car drove by and a lady waved at me. When she waved at me, I smiled for the first time in a long time. A feeling of joy and happiness suddenly filled my heart and just like that, again I felt something I have not felt in a long time, hope. I dropped the knife, went inside to eat and forgot all about what I was about to do.

> You do not have to be a licensed missionary or have a title in order for you to share the Word of God!

I wish that lady was here so that I could hug her and tell her that she saved my life."

A lady stood up in the audience and walked to the front and they both hugged and stayed hugging while crying.

Listen to me, you do not have to be a licensed missionary or have a title in order for you to share the Word of God in order for you to simply show kindness to someone, just don't overlook an opportunity to do so. Most times anyway, titles rarely represent the person who they really are.

You have been taught the Bible from childhood, even if you only know the very basics about the life of Christ, you are a qualified disciple, commissioned to go out beyond the four walls of the church! Did you not know that there is life beyond the four walls of the church, it's about relationships with people beyond the church even beyond the community.

The word disciple originated from the Latin word "Discipulus" meaning "Student." It's derived from the root word meaning, "To learn." In its noun form "Disciple" means "A personal follower of Jesus, a student of a teacher, leader or philosopher."

We find in the book of Matthew where Jesus urged His disciples to "Go and make disciples of all the nations, baptizing them in the name of the Father and the son and

> God is looking for Kingdom Vesseled Disciples!

the Holy Spirit. Teach these new disciples to obey all the commands I have given you. And be sure of this: I am with you always, even to the end of the age" (Matt. 28:19-20 kjv).

Like I mentioned earlier, God is not looking for more churches, neither is He looking for more preachers or pastors. God wants you and I to graduate into His kingdom and is looking for Kingdom Vesseled Disciples!

These were very high expectations and probably would seem impossible to fulfil so Jesus reminded His disciples that He would be with them always because they would always need to be with Him!

Apostle Paul, a Christian leader and perhaps considered to be one of the most important persons to follow Jesus was also probably one of the greatest disciples of Christ during his life but it did not all start out that way.

We find in (Acts 9:1-3 kjv), Apostle Paul who was called Saul (Acts 13:9 kjv) traveling through Damascus searching out all the Christians and the disciples so that he could bound, persecute, and basically kill them all. A light from heaven shined around him so bright that it made him fall to the ground.

He heard a voice saying to him, "Saul, Saul why persecutest me?" (Acts 9:5 kjv) Saul not recognizing the voice of the Lord asked, "Who

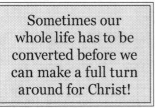

Sometimes our whole life has to be converted before we can make a full turn around for Christ!

art thou, Lord?" And Jesus replied, "I am Jesus whom thou persecutes." Saul said, "Lord, what wilt thou have me to do?" And the Lord said, "Arise, and go into the city, and it shall be told thee what thou must do (Acts 9:6 kjv). From that point on Saul also called Paul became a disciple of Christ. I tell you that sometimes our whole life has to be converted before we can make a full turn around for Christ.

There will come times throughout our life when we will have to go through difficult situations before the Lord is fully able to use us. The Lord will allow Trials and hardships to occur in our lives because He knows that they will only make us stronger and prepare us for future situations and that He will reveal Himself to us anyway and anywhere He chooses.

Remember, He was the Burning bush on the mountain, remember, He was the Veil in the temple, remember, He was the Fourth Man in the fiery furnace, He was the Mercy Seat in the old testament and remember, He was the Voice that told Joshua to, "Be thou not afraid, neither be thou dismayed: for the Lord thy God is with thee withersoever thou goest!"

Just because The Lord was seen differently to man in the Old Testament than in the New Testament does not mean He has changed, He is still the same God.

God himself, has equipped and given you and I the same authority to do miraculous things. He said, "Go in my name, raise the dead and cast out the kingdom of darkness." We are hearers and doers but, You Lord will be glorified and your name glorified above any other name!

We have been equipped to lead people to Christ that they may be saved, given the power to heal the sick, to cast out demons and as a Vessel for Christ you my friend can-not be afraid because, in you is greater than he that is in the world so you can operate within boundaries on His behalf! Therefore, we as Christians have been given the duty as being a disciple of Christ, to go out and make disciples of everyone and teaching them to obey His commandments! Remember this:

"You are now entering the mission field."

Reflection and Relevant Questions

1. In this chapter, we talked about Saul traveling on his way to Damascus with the intentions of destroying the church and the Christians there. God said, "Saul, Saul why persecuted me?" Why do you think that God was referring to Himself as opposed to the Jews, the church and the Christians whom he was going to persecute?

2. In what ways are you not only preparing yourself to be an effective vessel for Christ here on earth, but more importantly preparing yourself for the kingdom?

3. In this chapter, Paul mentioned the phrase, "You are now entering the mission field." What does this phrase mean to you?

    a. Name a time in your life when it seemed like life was at a total standstill and hope for you was bottomed out but, God stepped in and did a complete turnaround and you were used as a vessel for Christ.

CONCLUSION

t was standing room only. Every television around the world was tuned in. Even members of other teams had gathered around the track with eyes focused on one team and one person in particular. The year was 1956. The cost of a new car averaged around $15,000. January of that same year Elvis Presley released his first hit, "Heartbreak Hotel."

It was the beginning of The 1956 Summer Olympics held in Melbourne Australia and the race was the 4x100 meter relay. I love the 4x100 meter relay race because it is fast, but the fastest runners are not guaranteed a win. The key to this event is based on how much time spent during the exchanging of the baton. Each runner in the 4x100 relay race is to deliver the baton as quickly as possible to the next runner but what's equally important to the time spent exchanging the baton is the accuracy of the person delivering the baton, the one who is handing the baton off to the next person.

The third leg of that 1956 U.S. 4x100 meter relay team was a young lady named Wilma Glodean Rudolf Nicknamed "Skeeter" for her famous speed.

At the 1956 Olympics, Wilma Rudolph was considered one of the fastest woman in the world. But before she considered the Olympics or even running for that matters, Wilma Rudolf had many obstacles to endure. As a child, she was afflicted with double pneumonia, scarlet fever and polio and had problems with of all things her left leg causing her to wear a leg brace but through self-determination and will power she became a major vessel on the US 4x100meter Olympic relay team.

With her long arm stretched behind her and one leg stretched forward Wilma Rudolph anxiously waited for her teammate who was quickly approaching her to hand her the baton. With the noise from the crowd and even from other runners, Wilma only wanted to hear those two distinct words they had practiced with for months, "Go and Get it." Wilma Rudolph screamed waving her teammate towards her, "Come on bring me the baton!" While she anxiously waited, she thought about everything she had experienced in life that had tried to hinder her from getting to this point, as a child suffering paralysis in her legs, the many days watching from a window children playing when she could not, poverty, polio, double pneumonia, discouragement beating her down from every angle.

With the whole world watching, Wilma thought to herself, No way am I going to let my country, my teammates or myself down! Without looking back at her teammate who was quickly approaching, she heard the first word, "Go!" And with that Wilma took off running with a burst of speed. Her teammate screamed out again, "get it!" Running at top speed Wilma reached her long arm behind her and grabbed the baton from her teammate and with all she had within her she passed the runner in front of her and their team won first place in that heat. Out of the fifty-seven nations participating in the 1956 Olympics, USA came out on top winning a bronze medal in the 4x100 relay, what an achievement! Mrs. Rudolph ran the third leg for a specific reason. If their team was behind, Wilma Rudolph could catch up with them and if another runner was in front of her, she could pass them up. In addition to being the fastest she could deliver the baton with precise accuracy not losing a second in the exchange. Without having a fast and effective deliverer, the delivery of anything can at times become meaningless.

When you think of a delivery service, businesses like Uber, Door

Dash and UPS quickly comes to mind. But what about the deliverer, the one who steps out of the car or truck and delivers the package to its destination? If they are a slow deliverer and inefficient, the whole company will fall apart. It's all about the deliverer.

When you look at it from a spiritual aspect, God has a delivery service in mind for us as a deliverer. We are God's personal delivery service. We were designed to be human Spiritual Vessels who will carry and deliver His Word and His promises to the World.

If you are to be an effective deliverer of His Word, you must first be in alignment with Him. Think about it this way. When a car is properly in alignment, it gets better mileage and you get better performance. When we get into the place of alignment with God, we are able to step into our Calling in becoming a Vessel unto Honor which He desires thus fulfilling our purpose and His promises will become inevitable. We were made to walk with Him and our connection with Him is all directly related to being in relational alignment with Him.

You can possess the highest of degrees owning huge corporations feeling you have it all, but I am here to tell you that you will never be able to fully step into your calling until you have intimacy with Jesus. Being a Vessel unto Honor means that we are in direct proportion with Christ and that you are coming into a position of submission and agreement with Him. Our hearts are right with Him and our spirit soul and body is working together in peace and harmony.

The Lord is saying to you at this very moment my dear reader, "You did not choose me, but I chose you and appointed you that you should go and bear fruit, and that your fruit should remain, that whatever you ask the father in my name He may give you"(John 15:16 kjv).

As you look over your life, ask yourself, "Lord, how can I savor this moment and become that deliverer that Vessel You have called me to be?" Answer, Simply ask. The Bible says, "Ask, and it shall be given you; seek, and ye shall find; knock, and it shall be opened unto you:"(Matt: 7:7 kjv). Solomon asked God for understanding:

"Give therefore thy servant an understanding heart to judge thy people, that I may discern between good and bad"(1 Kings 3:9 KJV).

And God gave Solomon more than what he asked for, wisdom. Only thing necessary for you to do is to simply "Ask" and you will receive the knowledge and understanding on how God can use you as His personal deliverer and as a Vessel of Honor!

You are a chosen generation, a royal nation a peculiar people whom He has called out of darkness into His marvelous light to do great works. God has given you permission to go out to the world. You my friend, are on the mission field right now, so gird up your loins, and let's get to work!

SCRIPTURE INDEX

TO CONTACT THE AUTHOR

I pray that this book has been a blessing to you and through Christ Jesus has encouraged and inspired you. I would love to hear from you as you strengthen your walk with Christ.

PLEASE CONTACT ME AT:

Phillips772004@yahoo.com

OTHER TITLES FROM THE AUTHOR

1. FROM TRIALS TO BLESSINGS (2007)
2. EMBRACED (2012)
3. IN HIS PRESENCE (2014)
4. THE PURPLE APPLE (2015)
5. RESERVATIONS FOR THE KINGDOM, PLEASE (2018)
6. OVERCOMING THE STORMS (2020)

Paul Phillips
ISBN 978-1-4343-0561-9

Be blessed, and know that your blessings are just a prayer away. Paul Phillips tells the true story of being in a coma for seven days. During that time, God allowed Paul's spirit to visit and experience Heaven. He tells of healing experiences of the spiritual and physical body, mind and soul through the power of Prayer. Come with him as he: *Tells of his experience in HEAVEN!!*Tells of being greeted by loved ones!*Tells of indescribable sights & sounds there!*Tells of experiencing unspeakable joy & happiness! *Tells how your trials can be turned into a blessing!*Tells of the feeling of love by God's presence & more!

Paul Phillips
ISBN: 978-1-4685-4178-6

"Embraced" is the story of a boy named Taylor Mitchell growing up in present day Kansas. Taylor lives with his seemingly strict and disciplinary father and feels that life is unbearable and hard. It is not until Taylor accidentally finds his father's journal he wrote regarding growing up in the 1950's and 1960's that he realizes that his life was not as bad as he thought it was.

Paul Phillips

ISBN 9781491843321

If you have ever wondered what it means or how to get into the presence of the Lord, this book is for you. In this book you will not only learn how to allow to recognize His presence but also how to receive and enjoy the many blessings set aside just for you.

Paul Phillips
ISBN 9781504911122

The Purple Apple is about a boy who moves into a new neighborhood and finds himself constantly being bullied by two of the toughest boys in the school. But, by being bullied, he and his friends accidently finds a cure that just in the nick of time saves the entire neighborhood from a sudden illness. You will enjoy reading this book. It will inspire you and put a smile on your face. Most of all, it reminds us all that one person can make a difference! You will discover the secret of the Purple Apple, The real Me. Carton and the true meaning of friendship.

Paul Phillips
ISBN 978-1-5462-3317-6(sc)
ISBN 978-1-5462-3316-9(e)

Here are keys to unlock the kingdom of heaven! With encouragement, life experiences, and biblical guidance, Minister and Author Paul Phillips brings to you, "Reservations for the Kingdom, Please!" He gives an insight and areas you need to focus on, pray about, and live accordingly in order to receive blessings of that kingdom. Minister Phillips reveals how to recognize God's voice, keep a good name, be transformed, be an effective listener and live according to God's word. Whatever situation you may be experiencing just remember that you still have keys and rights to the kingdom of heaven! Heaven was and is prepared just for you!

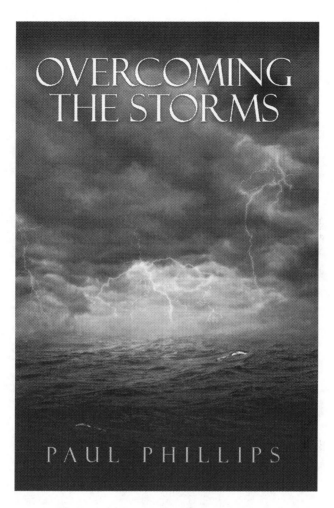

Paul Phillips

ISBN: 9781728369983

Do you feel that life has overwhelmed you to the point to where you simply want to throw in the towel? Get encouraged as Minister Paul Phillips uses God's servants from the Holy Bible, world events and personal experiences to show that even when going through the worst possible storms of life, they can be overcome! You may be going through the toughest storms and battles in your life, but these are the times when we need to take our eyes off of ourselves and look to the one who has all power to heal! Yes, you are an overcomer and God is the healer.

Printed in the United States
by Baker & Taylor Publisher Services